PICTORIAL HISTORY

OF THE

SECOND WORLD WAR

A PHOTOGRAPHIC RECORD
OF ALL THEATERS OF ACTION
CHRONOLOGICALLY ARRANGED

VOL. 1

New York
WM. H. WISE and CO., INC.
1944

PRINTED IN THE UNITED STATES OF AMERICA
AMERICAN BOOK—STRATFORD PRESS, INC., NEW YORK

FOREWORD

THE most prodigious war in history has provided the reader with an inestimable quantity of photographic record. In addition to the customary industry of the news agencies, the belligerent governments have applied themselves to the accumulation of fabulous picture files. In the United States, Great Britain and Russia, each branch of service has an extensive corps of expert photographers. The enemy nations have indicated a similar fecundity, although it has perhaps been on not so comprehensive a basis.

THE PICTORIAL HISTORY OF THE SECOND WORLD WAR in its two volumes has attempted to present a selection of the best of this photography. Unlike most picture books of the war, the material has been arranged in chronological order so that the reader is provided with a running story with all events in their true sequence. In a war of so many complexities, with critical campaigns occurring simultanously in many parts of the globe, this feature will serve to clarify incidents that over a four-year period have become obscure and remote.

Oddly enough, despite the diligence of the photographer historians, a few of the important and dramatic events have been missed. For instance, during the famous Altmark incident there were no photographs taken. This may be ascribed either to the absence of a camera man or to the rapid dramatic action which did not permit picture shooting. In these few cases, the publishers have substituted an artist's conception of the scene, based on eyewitness stories.

As picture editor the publishers were fortunate to secure the services of Al E. Davies of the New York *Herald Tribune*. Mr. Davies selected the pictures and edited the captions.

To provide the reader with a simplified arrangement, the volumes have been divided into sections, each of which pictorially reports one year of the war. Preceding each division is a short chronology of the important military developments from which have been excluded political interpretation and brash prognostication. It is felt that the written chronology will supply a pattern in which the subsequent pictures may be mentally filed and catalogued.

THE PUBLISHERS

THE FIRST YEAR

THE storm which had been brewing over Europe broke on September 1, 1939, when German troops crossed their eastern frontier and invaded Polish soil.

Since 1936, when she sent her troops into the Rhineland, Germany had executed each step of a carefully calculated plan, the ultimate objective of which was the regaining of her position as one of the world's great powers. The occupation of the Rhineland, previously demilitarized by the treaty of Versailles, was the first overt act. Then came the bloodless annexation of Austria in 1938, and the mockery of the Munich Pact which gave the Sudetenland to the Reich in the same year. In the Spring of 1939 she took the rest of Czechoslovakia, an appropriation which resulted in no display of resistance by either France or Great Britain. In August she effected the non-aggression pact with Russia which temporarily removed the threat of a two-front war and completed her preparations for the subjugation of Poland.

The march into Poland was introduced by the familiar Nazi preamble. Hitler told the German people that the Poles had refused all offers of peace, had persecuted the German population of Poland, and had violated the common frontier. The British Blue Book, which was published a few weeks after the hostilities, reported an entirely different story. It told of the many meetings of Sir Nevile Henderson, the British Ambassador to Berlin, with German foreign minister Joachim Von Ribbentrop. Held during the days immediately preceding the invasion, these interviews had established that war was inevitable unless Poland agreed to certain territorial concessions. Hitler and Von Ribbentrop expressed themselves as resentful of England's "interference" in the form of the Anglo-Polish alliance and her attempt to "bargain" over Germany's vital interests.

Future historians will record that when the meticulous preparations of the Reich war machine were completed, not even Poland was given the chance to "bargain." On August 31, Von Ribbentrop gave Sir Nevile the text of sixteen proposals which represented the German demand. Briefly outlined they were:

GERMAN DEMANDS

THE free city of Danzig was to be given to the Reich; Gdynia to remain Polish; the fate of the Polish corridor to be decided within twelve months by a plebiscite under international supervision; only those resident in the region before January 1, 1918, were to be permitted to vote (this would automatically insure a plurality in favor of Germany); until the plebiscite both Germany and Poland were to have free access to certain roads in the Corridor; if the Corridor voted for Poland, Germany was to have a corridor across it to East Prussia; if the region fell to Germany, there was to be an exchange of populations; complaints of the minorities were to be submitted to an international commission.

When the Polish ambassador attempted that day to relay the plan to Warsaw he found that communications had been cut. The German government broadcast the proposals, and when no answer was received from Warsaw, the first German blitzkrieg went into action. Great Britain and France, true to the terms of their alliance with Poland, declared war on Germany, and the holocaust of the world was under way.

The story of the military operations in Poland is one of brave, futile resistance against a highly-geared war machine trained in new methods. In the years during which the rest of Europe had attempted to stave off the inevitable through appeasement, Germany had been piecing together her military thunderbolt. Her bombing planes softened up the antiquated Polish fortifications and blasted away at the key cities. Her mechanized divisions gobbled up huge areas of the flat terrain of Poland with amazing speed. One by one the cities of Czestochowa, Katowice, Cracow, Gdynia, Kutno and Brest-Litovsk fell in order. The German high command announced on September 23 that the Polish campaign was over, although the capital of Warsaw did not surrender until September 27.

The full significance of the German-Russian pact signed in August was revealed on September 16 when the Soviet government notified Warsaw it could no longer regard the Polish state as existing. Russian troops moved westward into Poland, and on September 28, Foreign Commissar V. M. Molotov and Von Ribbentrop signed an agreement partitioning Poland for the fourth time in its history.

RUSSIAN-FINNISH WAR

ON November 28, after a brief wrangle during which Russian demands that Finland cede certain territory in the Karelian Isthmus were denied, diplomatic relations between the two countries were broken. The United States government offered to mediate the dispute, but by November 30, Russia's land, air and sea forces had gone into action. For the first two months of the struggle, the Finns put up a magnificent fight. The Mannerheim Line in Karelia proved stronger than the Soviet had anticipated, while in the north Finnish ski troops deployed in a type of guerrilla warfare that kept the Russian army constantly off balance. But, gradually the Russians brought to bear the weight of its vast resources of manpower and armament. The small Finnish air force was gradually eliminated, and Russian bombers were able to pound at will the Mannerheim fortifications. Finland finally gave up and signed a treaty of peace at Moscow on March 12, 1940.

The price she paid was the secession of the Karelian Isthmus, including the eastern islands on the Gulf of Finland, the City of Viipuri and the region around Lake Ladoga; parts of the communes of Kuusamo and Salla; the western section of the Rybachi peninsula on the Arctic Sea; a lease to Russia for 30 years of the Hango Peninsula.

WAR IN THE WEST

THUS far operations in the west had been so limited that American journalists began to write about the "phony" war. With the exception of minor skirmishes, French and German forces remained inactive on opposite sides of the Maginot Line. But on April 9 Germany opened her great assault by simultaneous movements into Denmark and Norway. Denmark's King Christian recognized the futility of his position and immediately ordered his subjects to submit. In Norway, Germany struck at several points. Troop transports accompanied by the main units of the German Navy steamed through the Kattegat and Skagerrak. Here they met the British and French fleets in engagements costly to both sides. It has since been estimated that Germany lost one-third of her naval power in the Skagerrak and along the Norwegian Atlantic coastline. But her objective was accomplished when she forced landings at Oslo, Stavanger, Bergen and Narvik.

The surprise nature of the attack and the treachery of Norway's Vidkun Quisling gave the important initial advantages to the German forces. The British did manage to land forces at Aandalsnes, Namsos, Trondheim, and the Narvik area. But by May 8, most of the British forces had been withdrawn, and in June the last of the British left Narvik.

On May 10, Germany struck at France in a pattern which closely followed that of World War I. Skirting the Maginot Line she sent her troops through Holland, Belgium and Luxemburg. British forces, already established in France, went into Belgium to fight at the side of King Leopold's troops. On May 14, the Dutch surrendered after their army and civilian population had taken an unmerciful pounding. On May 28, King Leopold capitulated to prevent bloodshed in a hopeless cause. By this time the German mechanized divisions had crossed the French border at Sedan and were making their way towards the Channel ports. They captured Boulogne May 25, Calais May 26, and now had the British bottled in Flanders with Dunkirk presenting the only avenue of escape.

By June 4, the British had accomplished the historic evacuation of Dunkirk. They had succeeded in the impossible of safely ferrying 330,000 out of a possible 400,000 troops to England. In facing alone the German war machine, the French assumed a hopeless task. Paris fell on June 14 and, on June 22, France surrendered and signed the armistice terms at Compiegne.

Meanwhile Italy had gained much doubtful fame by declaring war on France and Great Britain on June 10, a date when the defeat of France was assured. During the remaining few days of French resistance, Italian troops deployed along the French border in an ineffectual manner which earned her some minor territorial awards at the armistice.

It was not until August that Italy made her first real play in the Axis combination. In a campaign broadly calculated to take the Suez Canal and thus cut England's life line, her forces in Libya and Italian East Africa went into action. Her East African units took British Somaliland on August 17, and on September 16 the zenith in the drive out of Libya was reached in the capture of Sidi Barrani.

TWENTY-ONE YEARS OF PEACE ENDS. In a broadcast to the world from No. 10 Downing Street at 11:15 A. M. Sunday September 3, 1939, Prime Minister Neville Chamberlain said: "This morning the British Ambassador in Berlin handed the German government a final note stating that unless we heard from them by eleven o'clock that they were prepared at once to withdraw their troops from Poland a state of war would exist between us, I have to tell you now that no such undertaking has been received and that consequently this country is at war with Germany. . . . Now may God bless you all. May He defend the right. It is the evil things that we shall be fighting against—brute force, bad faith, injustice, oppression and persecution—and against them I am certain that the right will prevail."

WAR COMES TO BRITAIN. Anxious faces lined the pavement in Downing Street on that eventful Sunday as Mr. Chamberlain, in the Cabinet Room of No. 10, began his broadcast. Almost as he finished speaking the wail of air raid sirens all over the country electrified the already tense atmosphere. Londoners, expecting bombs to drop, made their way into the shelters in quiet and orderly groups. It was a false alarm, and soon the sirens sounded the "raiders passed" signal, but no declaration of war could have been more dramatic.

FIRST SUBMARINE SINKING. Within a few hours of the outbreak of war a German U-Boat claimed its first victim. With no warning, the liner "Athenia," bound from Belfast to Montreal with more than 1,000 passengers many of whom were women and children, was torpedoed in the Atlantic. All but 112 were picked up by ships which hurried to her assistance. As a number of the passengers were Americans, the German propaganda department put out the story that a British submarine, on Winston Churchill's order, had committed the deed to influence American opinion. The "Athenia" is seen settling down by the stern.

GERMAN ARTILLERY MOVES UP. To economize their stocks of gasoline the Germans used thousands of horse-drawn vehicles to follow up the advance of their mechanized units during the Polish campaign. Here a German gun team, crossing a river by one of the few intact bridges, seems to be finding the Polish road, churned up by their own tanks and armored cars, difficult to negotiate.

POLISH INFANTRY ATTACKING. In spite of their great fighting qualities and powers of endurance, the Polish Army could do little to check the swift advance of the enemy's armored columns. Nevertheless they faced with courage a tremendously superior enemy in an heroic attempt to defend their homeland. The picture shows Polish infantry charging forward to the attack.

POLISH FORTRESS BATTERED INTO SUBMISSION. For six days and nights the 11-inch guns of the German battleship "Schleswig-Holstein" bombarded the Polish fort of Westerplatte, on the outskirts of Danzig, at point-blank range (right) whilst from the land and air furious assaults were made by large and well-equipped German forces. For six days the Poles held out, but on the morning of the seventh the commander of the garrison surrendered to save what were left of his men. It was estimated that the German land forces alone amounted to a division, whereas the defenders, all told, numbered only a company. The picture above shows the Nazi flag being hoisted by German soldiers over the shell-torn battlements after the garrison surrendered.

After twenty-five years: a British expeditionary force lands in France

B.E.F. LANDS IN FRANCE. The plans for the transportation of men and material to France had been drawn up by the French and British General Staffs long before the war clouds broke, so that when war was declared it only remained to put them into operation. With great speed—and even greater secrecy—men, guns, tanks and all the equipment and supplies necessary to maintain an army in the field, were shipped across the Channel, and it was not until September 12, by which time most of the material had safely arrived, that the British public were let into the secret. The picture on the right shows troops and guns being disembarked at a French port. Above is seen Viscount Gort, V.C., who was appointed Commander-in-Chief of the British armies in France, under supreme command of General Maurice Gustave Gamelin.

THE COURAGEOUS GOES DOWN. H.M. Aircraft Carrier Courageous was struck amidships by a torpedo from a German submarine while on patrol duty on September 17 and sank within a very short time. Orders to abandon ship were given five minutes after she was struck, but her commander, Captain Mackeig-Jones

(in circle) remained on the bridge to the end and went down with his ship. The picture shows the "Courageous" heeling over shortly before her death plunge; her crew can be clearly seen scrambling down the side into the water. The Courageous had a full complement of 1,126 officers and men, of whom 515 lost their lives.

HORRORS OF INVADED POLAND. The horrors of modern aerial warfare are forcefully illustrated by this picture of a Warsaw boy squatting miserably among the wreckage of what was his home. Scenes such as this were common all over Poland where the Nazi air force rained death and destruction on countless open towns and brought untold misery and hardship to Poland's civilian population. In spite of constant raids, however, and the indiscriminate damage they wrought, the morale of Poland's civilians remained unshaken.

GERMAN ADVANCE IN POLAND. Simultaneously from four sides Hitler's forces marched towards Warsaw, and as the endless lines of vehicles made their way through the countryside, villages (as in the picture above) and farmhouses (below) were reduced to shapeless heaps of rubble. The Poles hoped in vain that the autumn rains would hold up the onrush, but their hopes were mocked by cloudless skies, and the occupation of Western Poland, for which Hitler's time-table had allowed a month, took little more than a week.

GERMAN TROOPS FIGHTING IN WARSAW'S SUBURBS. Masses of mechanized forces, hundreds of bombing planes, working together in close co-operation, were the primary reason for German successes in Poland. Yet, despite the Poles' enormous inferiority in both these arms, it was a month before the Germans forced the capital to surrender. These two pictures illustrate the final phase of Warsaw's resistance. Above, German artillery, powerfully supported by tanks, is seen battering its way through the streets on the outskirts of the city. Below, infantry are advancing along a street, blocked by trolley cars, under cover of tanks.

BOMBED POLISH ARMORED TRAIN. This remarkable picture shows what happened to a Polish armored train attacked by a Nazi bomber. High explosive bombs weighing 520 lb. were used in the attack; their destructive effect can be gathered from the damage to the train itself as well as from the size of the bomb crater.

WARSAW'S RESISTANCE ENDS. On September 15 the Germans claimed to have surrounded Warsaw, but it was not until the 27th that the capital, battered by aerial and artillery bombardment, was forced to capitulate. On that day, high officials of the Polish and German armies met in a bus on the outskirts of the

Polish garrison leaves the devastated city   September 30, 1939

capital and arranged terms of surrender (in circle). Three days later the remnants of the heroic Polish garrison marched out of the city, which was occupied by Nazi troops. The above picture shows the disarmed soldiers marching dejectedly out of the capital they had so bravely defended, watched by civilians.

A NEW DIVISION OF POLAND. Poland was again divided amongst her neighbors when on September 29, German Foreign Minister Ribbentrop in Moscow signed a second Soviet-German agreement defining the boundaries of the German and Soviet occupied areas of the country. The map (right) shows how the territory was divided. Above, V. M. Molotov, Russian Premier, signs the agreement on behalf of the Soviets. Behind him stand Ribbentrop and Marshal Stalin. Germany took not only Danzig and the Polish Corridor, but Warsaw and vast areas to the south which had never had any German population. Russia limited her claims to the area east of Brest-Litovsk, an area predominantly Ukrainian, and almost identical with that bounded by the famous "Curzon Line." This line had been suggested as the frontier between Poland and Russia by Lord Curzon in 1920. Germany secured all the coal mines and industrial areas, while Russia obtained the Galicia oilfields.

NAZI CONQUERORS IN SILENT WARSAW. On October 5 Hitler flew to Warsaw to take the salute at the Grand Review of his victorious troops. The route was carefully chosen to avoid those parts of the city that had been devastated by aerial bombardment, and the streets were lined by Nazi troops to keep the crowds in check. This precaution, however, seemed unnecessary since Warsaw's population stayed indoors, and the procession made its way through almost deserted streets, as can be seen above.

FRENCH AND GERMAN PATROLS AT WORK. Although during the first few months of the war there were no large scale operations on the Western Front, patrols from both sides were constantly seeking information concerning the strength and disposition of the opposing forces. Above, a French patrol moves cautiously through a shell-torn village, while (below) Germans are seen engaged on a similar errand.

ROYAL OAK TORPEDOED. By a feat of great daring and skill, to which Winston Churchill himself paid tribute, a German U-boat, under the command of Lieutenant Prien, penetrated the defenses of Scapa Flow and torpedoed the battleship H.M.S. Royal Oak on October 14. "It appears probable," said Mr. Churchill, speaking to the House of Commons on October 17, as First Lord of the Admiralty, "that the U-boat fired a salvo of torpedoes of which only one hit the bow. Twenty minutes later the U-boat fired three or four torpedoes, and these, striking in quick succession, caused the ship to capsize and sink." The Royal Oak, a ship of 29,000 tons, had a main armament of eight 15-in. guns. Eight hundred and ten British seamen lost their lives. Berlin acclaimed it as a triumph, and Prien and his crew were given a well-staged reception.

German planes raid the Firth of Forth

THE WAR COMES TO SCOTLAND. On October 16 an ineffective attack was launched by German war-planes upon British warships in the Firth of Forth. The above photograph, taken from one of the enemy machines, was published upside down in a Berlin illustrated paper, and purported to show a bomb bursting on the bridge. The "bomb explosion," which can be seen just to the left of the center pier, is, in reality, Inch Garvie Island upon which the pier is built. Although the raid was carried out by twelve or fourteen

enemy bombers only very slight damage was done to three British ships, the cruisers Southampton and Edinburgh, and the destroyer Mohawk. German aircraft had flown over Rosyth to reconnoiter earlier in the morning, and the first of the series of actual raids began about 2.30 in the afternoon and continued until 4 p.m., when the last of the German planes was chased away by R.A.F. fighters. Only two civilian casualties were reported and the railway continued its normal service over the bridge uninterruptedly. Four enemy planes were brought down. The picture above shows an enemy plane being driven off by anti-aircraft fire after dropping a bomb near H.M.S. Edinburgh. On the right is the funeral of two of the Nazis killed in the raid.

U.S. SENATE REPEALS EMBARGO. On October 27, after more than a month of fierce debate, the U.S. Senate voted for the repeal of the embargo on war materials that formed a part of America's Neutrality Law. This meant that belligerent countries could purchase war materials from America only if they paid for them in cash and carried them in their own ships. Above, President Roosevelt is seen urging repeal of the embargo in a message to a joint session of the Congress. The effect of repeal was to place American war production at the disposal of the Allies; the blockade precluded Germany from buying in America.

AIR AID FROM AMERICA. The repeal of America's Neutrality Law enabled the Allies to order aircraft from American firms, and on the very day that the Bill was signed orders amounting to approximately $220,000,000 for planes and equipment were confirmed. Above, reconnaissance bombers from the Lockheed Company's California factory receiving final touches. Below, a Navy dive bomber is being towed across the border into Canada, as is required by American neutrality regulations, for shipment to Great Britain.

The Munich beer hall explosion

ATTEMPT ON LIFE OF HITLER. On November 8, Hitler unexpectedly decided to attend a meeting held in the Buergerbraukeller, a beer hall in Munich, to celebrate the anniversary of the Nazi putsch of 1923. After making a violently anti-British speech, he left the building at 9:15 p.m. together with all the more important of the Nazi personalities who had accompanied him. Twenty minutes later a bomb, which had been concealed in one of the supporting pillars, shattered the building, causing the ceiling to collapse on the

assembly, which included many of Hitler's earliest supporters. Nine people were killed, and more than sixty injured. The German authorities accused the British Secret Service of responsibility for the plot; large rewards were offered for information, and workmen who had prepared the hall and others, arrested; but whether this was a genuine attempt on the Fuehrer's life, or just another "stunt" to increase his popularity, we may never know. Hitler is seen speaking (left) and damage done by the bomb is seen above.

END OF A GERMAN SUBMARINE. Despite all Germany's efforts during the first few months of the war, her U-boats were never able to enjoy their success of the last war. New methods of detection enabled the Royal Navy to take a steady toll of the underwater raiders. In the early months Germany lost an average of three submarines a week. Most were lost without a trace, but in some cases British ships were able to rescue the crews. These pictures show a U-boat forced to the surface (above) and boats picking up survivors.

RUSSIA DECLARES WAR ON FINLAND. After consolidating her gains in Poland, Russia, for strategic reasons, made certain territorial demands on Finland, and when these were refused, launched her army and air force against that small country. Bombs fell on Helsinki, the capital, and other towns on the first day, and a stream of refugees fled across the frontier into Sweden. The pathetic picture above shows a sorrowing Finnish family taking a last look at their homeland before the train bears them into exile.

THE REDS COME TO FINLAND. Although most of the Russian air raids on Finland were directed against military objectives, it was inevitable that some of the bombs should miss their mark and inflict injury upon civilians and civilian property. Nevertheless, considering the number of bombs dropped, Finnish civilian casualties were surprisingly small. This was largely due to the efficiency of the Finnish A.R.P. Above is seen a block of flats in Helsinki which has been hit by a high explosive bomb and is blazing furiously.

A VICTIM OF THE NAZI RAIDER. Before the German commerce-raiding battleship was brought to book by the British Navy, she inflicted considerable loss to merchant shipping in the South Atlantic, the largest of her nine British victims being the 10,000-ton merchantman Doric Star captured and torpedoed on December 4. The picture shows an unnamed ship that met a similar fate being watched by the crew from the decks of the Admiral Graf Spee as the merchant ship heeled over preparatory to taking her death plunge.

The first great naval battle of the war

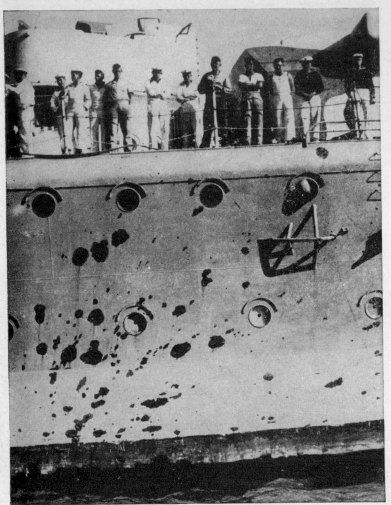

BATTLE OF THE RIVER PLATE. On Wednesday, December 13, a British squadron of three light cruisers, Exeter, Ajax and Achilles, commanded by Commodore Henry Harwood, was on patrol near the mouth of the River Plate. About 6 a.m. a German vessel was sighted and the British ships immediately attacked. It proved to be the German pocket battleship Admiral Graf Spee which had been preying on Allied shipping in those waters. She immediately opened fire on the Exeter, and after one or two ineffectual salvos scored a direct hit. She concentrated another turret on the Ajax and Achilles, but so skilfully were they maneuvered that they managed to keep out of harm's way. Before long the Exeter was reduced to one gun and forced to withdraw from the action. Although the German ship's armament was half as much again as the combined broadsides of the three British cruisers, Ajax and Achilles, using incredibly daring tactics, harried their more powerful opponent with such effect that she was forced to seek refuge in Montevideo Harbor in a damaged condition. Bottom left, Ajax seen from Achilles as she attacks; the smoke on the horizon marks the position of the German ship. Above, the Graf Spee is seen in Montevideo Harbor after the fight. Top left, the shell-scarred bows of the Graf Spee.

Last act of the River Plate battle—the Graf Spee scuttled

BURNING WRECK OF THE GRAF SPEE. By international law a belligerent warship in time of war may not stay in a neutral port for more than a specified time, and the whole world waited expectantly for the Graf Spee to come out of Montevideo and join battle again. Outside, the British ships lay in wait, anxious to finish the job they had so well begun. But it was not to be. On the evening of December 17, the Graf Spee steamed out of the harbor, but not, as was expected, to seaward, where the British ships lay in wait, but towards the west. Shortly after 8 p.m. two explosions shook the air and a flash of flame shot skyward. The ship was blotted from view by a

dense cloud of black smoke as she crumpled up, a mass of twisted steel. She had been scuttled by her commander on express orders from Hitler. Such was the inglorious end of one of the proudest ships of the German Navy. For his brilliant conduct of the battle Commodore Harwood (in circle left) received the K.C.B. and was promoted to rear-admiral. Captain Langsdorff (in circle right), the Graf Spee's commander, could not endure his shame; he died by his own hand two days after he had scuttled his ship. The picture above shows the blazing wreckage of the pocket battleship a short time after the charges had been fired by the crew of the German battleship.

The Germans scuttle the Columbus December 19, 1939

ATLANTIC LINER IN FLAMES. After being intercepted by a British warship about three hundred miles off the coast of Virginia on December 19, the liner Columbus, the third largest and one of the most luxurious vessels in the German merchant fleet, was set on fire by her crew to avoid capture. She belonged to the North-German Lloyd line and was a favorite with the American tourist trade. In the top picture she is seen blazing furiously from stem to stern. Below, her crew are seen taking to the boats.

A REVISED EMPIRE AIR SCHEME. A modification of the Empire Air Scheme in the Fall of 1939 provided that Australia should train most of her own air personnel, not in Canada but at home with the aid of instructors borrowed from Britain. The Commonwealth's new plan called for a contribution of 26,000 trained men to the Empire Air Forces within three years. On December 26 a first Australian air contingent landed in England. The picture shows them disembarking at a south coast port.

Some additions from the colonies to the B. E. F.

INDIANS AND CYPRIOTS ARRIVE IN FRANCE. Political controversy over "Dominion status" did not prevent the material expression of the overwhelming desire of the Indian people to take an active part in the struggle for freedom. Detachments of the Indian Army Service Corps, still a mainly unmechanized force, began to arrive in France at the end of 1939, where their columns of pack and draught mules afforded a valuable supplement to motor transport. The picture shows some of the drivers in camp in France.

One of the earliest of the smaller units of the Commonwealth to come forward with offers of help to Great Britain in her struggle was Cyprus, Britain's very loyal outpost in the Eastern Mediterranean. From the very beginning of hostilities recruits flocked to join the Cyprus R.A.S.C., and by the turn of the year a contingent of them had arrived in France with their mules (above) ready to assist in the transport of stores and similar duties with the various units of the B.E.F.

FROM NORTH OF THE BORDER. Canadian Air Force personnel made their first landings in Britain in the last two weeks of December, as an advance guard to prepare camps and training fields for the far larger number to follow—for in the last few months of 1939 seven thousand recruits, Canadian and American, had applied to join the Royal Canadian Air Force. The airmen in the picture, fresh from a training course in Canada, have just stepped ashore, and are acknowledging the welcome they found awaiting them.

ON THE FINNISH NORTHERN FRONT. One of the outstanding features of the Russo-Finnish War was the skill and audacity shown by the Finnish ski detachments (top). Each man was a master of the sport which had become an important wartime method of progression, and their agility and swiftness enabled them to penetrate far behind the enemy lines and harass their communications. The fearful cold in which the opposing armies had to fight is well illustrated by the frozen Russian corpses seen in the bottom picture.

LOSS OF H.M.S. GRENVILLE. On January 21, H.M. destroyer Grenville was sunk by mine or torpedo in the North Sea. There was no time to lower the boats, but other ships in the vicinity were able to rescue most of the crew. Altogether eight men were killed by the explosion, and seventy-three were reported missing and presumed dead. These two pictures show (top) the Grenville just before she took her final plunge; (below) a dramatic photograph of A. B. Bromfield, the last man to leave the ship, clinging to a porthole in the bows. The Grenville, a vessel of 1,485 tons, had a complement of 175 officers and men.

BIG GERMAN GUN IN ACTION. Although during the first few months of the war there was no large-scale activity on the Western Front, there were occasional artillery outbursts on both sides designed to draw the enemy fire and thereby give some indication of the artillery strength of the forces in the opposite sector. The Germans used a number of big guns on railway mountings such as that seen firing in the picture above. Their advantage was that they could be moved rapidly from one sector to another. Most of the fighting at this period took place in the Saar-Moselle region, south-east of the Luxembourg border.

SHELL-SCARRED EXETER COMES HOME. Bearing the scars of her encounter with the German pocket battleship, Admiral Graf Spee (see pages 39-43) off the River Plate, H.M.S. Exeter steamed into Plymouth, her home port, on February 15. She thus disproved the lie circulated widely by the Nazi propaganda department that she had been so badly damaged that she had had to be run aground to save her from sinking. The damage to her sides and funnels, although patched up and painted over, can be clearly seen.

ANZACS IN THE NEAR EAST. On February 12, the first contingent of Australian and New Zealand troops arrived at Suez to take up their stations for the defense of Palestine, Egypt and the Near East, and were welcomed by Anthony Eden, at that time Secretary of State for the Dominions. The model town seen above, with its neatly planned rows of tents and barracks was erected by native labor in three weeks.

The Altmark incident—H.M.S. Cossack to the rescue

GRAF SPEE AFTERMATH. During the early days of February the German tanker Altmark, which had acted as a supply ship to the ill-fated Graf Spee, was nearing the end of her perilous return voyage to Germany. On board she had 300 British seamen who had been captured from ships sunk by the Graf Spee. The British Admiralty decided that these men should be rescued and ordered the destroyer Cossack, under command of Captain Vian, to intercept the German ship. With the aid of aerial reconnaissance she was located and her position radioed to the Cossack, which intercepted her on the night of February 17, as she was steaming down the Norwegian coast. When the Altmark saw the British destroyer she sought shelter

in Joessing Fjord. Disregarding the fact that she was in Norwegian territorial waters, the Cossack followed her in, ran alongside, and her crew boarded the tanker. In the ensuing hand-to-hand fight seven of the German crew were killed but the British sailors were released. They had been held under hatches and had suffered terribly for several weeks. The captain of the Altmark had a fanatical hatred of everything English and his prisoners had suffered in consequence. The reconstruction on these two pages, specially drawn by Edgar Thurstan, shows the British boarding the Altmark to meet the German sailors and end the Altmark's short lived career as a prison ship of the Nazis.

HOME FROM A SAGA OF THE SEAS. After her successful expedition, H.M.S. Cossack returned to Britain with the sailors she had rescued from the Nazi prison ship Altmark. The Cossack is seen above approaching her dock at a Scottish port, her decks lined by her crew and the seamen she had rescued. An immense crowd had assembled on the dock to witness her triumphal return and gave her a tumultuous welcome.

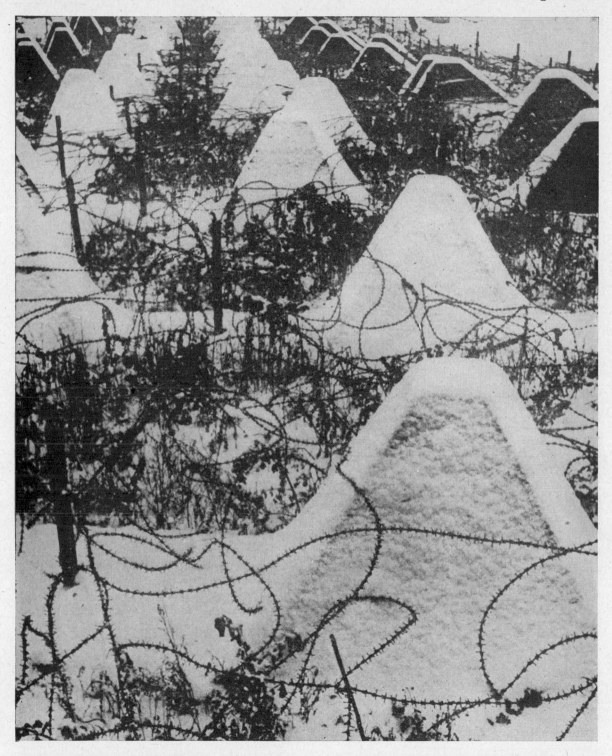

GERMAN DEFENSE SNOWBOUND. The desolate scene at the westwall of the Siegfried line, Germany's main defense sector. Facing the French Maginot Line, it is a continuous line running from Switzerland along the Rhine to Saarbruecken and up through Aix-la-Chapelle on the Belgian border. It is composed of two, three and sometimes four strings of forts, sometimes as deep as nine miles.

RIVER PLATE BATTLE HEROES HONORED. On February 23, London gave a tumultuous welcome to the officers and men of the cruisers Ajax and Exeter, victors of the battle against the German pocket battleship Admiral Graf Spee off Montevideo in December, 1939 (see pages 39-43). There was first a royal investiture at the Horse Guards Parade at which Rear Admiral Harwood, commander of the Exeter, received the K.C.B.

and other officers, petty officers and men who had shared in the action were decorated. Afterwards the men marched to the City where a ceremonial luncheon was given in their honor at the Guildhall and the Lord Mayor, Winston Churchill and others paid tribute to the Navy's latest exploit. In the picture on these pages the procession is passing Admiralty Arch between sidewalks jammed with cheering Londoners.

The British Prime Minister pays a visit to France   February, 1940

THE B.E.F. PASSES IN REVIEW. Prime Minister Neville Chamberlain and the British commander-in-chief, Lord Gort, watching a detachment of the British Army pass in review on a highway in France. The Prime Minister spent more than two weeks inspecting the troops, traveling up to the front and living with the Empire's soldiers and returned to England well pleased with the morale and condition of the allied forces.

NEW ZEALAND SAILORS HOME. New Zealand had a rousing welcome ready for her naval heroes when H.M.S. Achilles visited Auckland on February 23. As a unit of the New Zealand division, the cruiser had flown the Dominion's flag beside the white ensign at the Battle of the Plate, and 380 members of Captain Parry's gallant crew came from New Zealand. Achilles' deadly fire, unswerving as the Graf Spee's shells dropped all around her, had helped to speed the inglorious foe on her quest for safety in Montevideo.

RUSSIA AND FINLAND MAKE PEACE. For 104 days the Finns stood up to the enormous power of the Red Army. Then with their Mannerheim Line irretrievably breached they made peace. The terms differed from those offered by Russia before hostilities began chiefly in that no Russian territory was ceded in return for that seized. As seen on this map, Finland ceded the whole Karelian Isthmus, an area in Central Finland and part of the Rybachi Peninsula. (Inset) President Kallio is seen broadcasting the terms to the Finnish nation.

FINNS AND RUSSIANS MEET AT HANGOE. Besides losing Viborg, her most important port, Finland was forced to lease to Russia the peninsula of Hangoe, key to the Gulf of Finland. The lease was to run for thirty years at a yearly rental of about $150,000. The evacuation of the ceded areas began on March 14 and from Hangoe alone some 11,000 Finns departed, taking with them only such goods as they could carry. Above is the dramatic moment when three Russian soldiers first face a Finnish sentry across the new boundary.

SUMNER WELLES'S EUROPEAN TOUR. On February 25, Sumner Welles, U.S. Under-Secretary of State, and special envoy of President Roosevelt, arrived in Rome where he had the first of a series of exploratory talks on the European situation. Later he visited Berlin, Paris and London. The object of his visit was to gather first-hand information on the war situation for President Roosevelt. Above he is seen (left) with Viscount Halifax, then British Foreign Minister, later His Majesty's Ambassador to Washington.

HITLER AND MUSSOLINI MEET. The meeting between the German and Italian dictators at Brenner on March 18 aroused world-wide speculation. It was reported from Rome that it was in connection with a peace proposal of eleven points which Hitler had drawn up and shown to Sumner Welles. Mussolini, it was said, hoped to persuade the Fuehrer to modify them. In the light of later events, however, it seems much more probable that the meeting was to put the final touches to the agreement defining the role Italy was to play.

An Australian cruiser comes home

H.M.A.S. PERTH AT SYDNEY. The 7,000 ton cruiser of the Royal Australian Navy, to which she was presented by England, was welcomed on March 31, at Sydney, after she had steamed more than 52,000 miles since the outbreak of the war. She is seen (above) passing through the Panama Canal on her way to Australian waters. Below, some of her officers and men, their fixed bayonets gleaming in the sunlight, march through the streets of Sydney as Australian crowds pay homage.

A British destroyer goes down fighting April 8, 1940

H.M.S. GLOWWORM SUNK. On April 8, the British mine-laying destroyer, Glowworm, while carrying out duties off Norway, ran into a strong enemy force of destroyers and light cruisers and was sunk after a gallant fight. These pictures, taken from a Nazi warship, show (top) the destroyer laying a smoke screen immediately before she went down, and (below) oil-covered survivors being picked up by a German ship.

NAZI TROOPS LAND IN COPENHAGEN. The war, which had become practically a war of nerves since October, 1939, suddenly took a dramatic turn when in the early hours of April 9, Germany invaded Norway and Denmark. Here German troops are seen disembarking in Copenhagen from one of the many ships which ferried them across the Baltic. Meanwhile motorized units had invaded the country from the south. Denmark was unable to do more than protest at this flagrant violation of her territory. In a memorandum, Hitler attempted to justify his act by the claim that Britain and France were about to invade Scandinavia.

OCCUPATION OF NARVIK. Britain announced her intention on April 6 of mining Norwegian waters. This was used by Hitler as an excuse for his invasion of Norway. In fact his forces sailed before the British announcement and German destroyers entered Narvik Fjord on April 9. They torpedoed two Norwegian warships and disembarked stores and troops (top). Next day five British destroyers, led by Captain Warburton-Lee in H.M.S. Hardy, attempted recapture. They were driven back and Captain Warburton-Lee was killed, but they inflicted tremendous damage on enemy shipping as can be seen from the lower picture. Captain Warburton-Lee (inset) was posthumously awarded the Victoria Cross, Britain's highest honor.

THE SEIZURE OF OSLO. The occupation of the Norwegian capital was a masterpiece of treachery. For months Germany had been scheming with a group of Norwegian traitors led by Major Vidkun Quisling. The invasion was brilliantly planned and executed. All strategic points were occupied simultaneously. The Norwegians, ill-prepared for resistance, were dazed by the speed of the occupation and the paralysis of the machinery of government engineered by Quisling. The occupation of Oslo was typical, the forts in the

fjord were given orders not to fire and the electrically controlled mines were disconnected. Air raid alarms sounded but the Nazi planes dropped leaflets, not bombs. The population was further deceived by the arrival of military bands which played steadily for hours. Meanwhile tanks and guns had been poured into the city. The pictures show (top left) anti-aircraft gunner in the docks; (bottom left) tanks entering the city; (top right) a German military band playing and (bottom right) German troops receiving arms.

GERMAN CRUISER IN NORWEGIAN PORT. Hitler was prepared to pay any price for the speedy capture of Norway and flung the German Navy recklessly into the attempt. It suffered fearful losses from British submarines, surface ships and planes, which sank between them several capital ships and destroyers, but it achieved its purpose of diverting the British Navy's attention from German troopships and transports which were rushing men and ammunition into Norway as fast as they were able. This picture, taken in Trondheim Harbor, shows Nazi troops being disembarked by tender from a German heavy cruiser of the Hipper class. The German capture of Trondheim was to prove decisive in the struggle for Norway.

NAZI TANKS AND INFANTRY IN ACTION. Having consolidated their positions in Southern Norway, German troops pushed rapidly inland in order to join up with the troops from Bergen, Trondheim and elsewhere. Norway's small army could do little—the capture of the chief ports had disorganized mobilization and robbed it of its arsenals. Nevertheless, it fought gallantly against the invaders. The pictures show: (top) German infantry taking up positions on a lakeside road and tanks being ferried across a fjord.

THE R.A.F. RAIDS STAVANGER AND BERGEN. The Nazi occupation of Norway was not long to go unchallenged, and when on April 11, Winston Churchill promised that the Allies would aid Norway to the "best of their ability," R.A.F. bombers had already begun operations against the invader. From bases in Britain bomber squadrons launched a series of attacks on the German-occupied airfield at Stavanger, Norway's largest and most modern airfield. Their bombs wrought great damage both to the field and to enemy craft on the ground. The picture on the left, taken from one of the attacking planes, clearly shows

a bomb bursting near two enemy planes. Another bomb has hit the end of the concrete runway. Several more planes in the picture have been severely damaged. Craters on the field show where other bombs have fallen. The picture above shows an attack on German seaplanes anchored off Bergen. The white cigar-shaped object at the top left of the picture is a bomb falling close to the lens of the camera. The Germans gained a decisive advantage by occupying all the airfields in Norway, thus preventing the Allies from using fighter planes, so necessary to counteract the round-the-clock activity of the Nazi bombers.

ALLIES GO TO NORWAY'S AID. The help which the British government had promised to Norway was not long in forthcoming, and on April 15 it was announced that troops had made landings at several points and were establishing contact with the Norwegian forces. During the 400-mile voyage lifebelts were worn by the troops as seen in the picture below. The top picture shows a transport steaming into a Norwegian fjord. The landing was carried out without the loss of a single British ship or man, despite heavy attacks.

GERMANS ATTACK BRITISH TRANSPORTS AND BOMB NORWEGIAN TOWNS. As one of the British transports was nearing its destination British destroyers detected the presence of an enemy submarine and attacked it with depth charges which forced it to the surface in a damaged condition. The top picture shows the U-boat after the attack; the black dots in the water are members of the crew swimming away from the damaged submarine. The bottom picture shows a German warplane bombing the Norwegian town of Rena.

DIRECT HITS ON NAZI STORES IN NORWAY. On April 15, the R.A.F. carried out an extensive series of raids on Nazi supply centres. The picture above shows large wharf warehouses ablaze during a raid on Hardanger Fjord, near Bergen, where the Germans had established a base for their troops fighting in Southern Norway. During the whole of the Norwegian campaign bombers of the R.A.F. operating from Britain ceaselessly harried the Nazi communications with considerable success.

GERMANS PUSH ALLIES OUT OF LILLEHAMMER AND STEINKJER. British troops which had landed south of Trondheim joined up with the Norwegians fighting north of Oslo. Near Lillehammer they met powerful Nazi columns and, after fierce fighting, were forced to retire on April 25. Farther north, British troops pushing south from Namsos occupied Steinkjer, but had to retire on April 24 owing to enemy bombing. Pictures show German troops advancing towards Lillehammer (top) and (below) Steinkjer.

What the Nazis did to Namsos, Britain's chief base in Norway

BOMBING OF THE BRITISH BASE AT NAMSOS. Namsos, a pretty little Norwegian port situated at the head of the Namsen Fjord, north of Trondheim, was one of the places selected by the Allied High Command for landings in Norway. It became the main base for British forces operating against the Germans in the Trondheim area from the north, and from the moment the British arrived it was subjected to ceaseless bombardment from the air. At first the German airmen concentrated only on military stores and ammunition

dumps, but soon the whole town became a target, and its houses and churches were reduced to a shambles of blackened ruins and fallen masonry. It was here that Britain's lack of airfields in Norway was most keenly felt, for, being denied the use of fighter planes, there was nothing the troops could do to stave off the attacks, which in the end rendered the base untenable and forced the Allied forces to withdraw from Central Norway. This picture shows the desolation after high explosive and incendiary bombs fell.

GERMAN BOMBERS DESTROY BRITISH BASE. Aandalsnes, standing at the head of Romsdals Fjord, south of Trondheim, was another place chosen for Allied landings and, like Namsos, was the object of incessant bombing raids by the German Air Force from the moment the Allies arrived. It was from here, too, that the evacuation of Allied forces began on May 2. The picture above, showing clouds of smoke rising from the flaming town, gives some idea of the terrible conditions under which the evacuation was carried out.

BOMB DAMAGE IN NARVIK. Although the southern parts of Norway had been evacuated, fighting continued in the north. The mountainous character of the country with its deep valleys and pine woods, and its ragged coastline made Norway difficult for the Nazis to over-run. In the north Narvik became the main focus of war. The pictures above show (top) German transports and supply ships sunk in Narvik Harbor and (below) inhabitants driven from their homes by incendiary bombs which fell on the town.

Canadians mount guard at Buckingham Palace April 17, 1940

DOMINION TROOPS GUARD THEIR KING. The Canadian forces, whose first contingents with their commander, Major-General McNaughton, had arrived in England in December, 1939, received a signal honor four months later when they were called upon to take over guard duties at the royal palaces. The first to mount guard were the Toronto Scottish, whose band (above) is seen marching across the parade ground at their camp. Below, French Canadians of the First Division are marching up to Buckingham Palace.

CANADIANS FIGHT WITH BRITAIN. By the end of April Canada had called up almost 100,000 men. Canadian troops fought side by side with the British in Belgium and North France, a second division was nearly ready to go overseas and a third division was training in Canada. The Earl of Athlone, newly appointed governor general is shown (above) inspecting Canadian infantry in England on the eve of his departure for North America and (below) Canadian troops are seen training with field guns.

England's first taste of death from the sky

NAZI BOMBER CAUSES HAVOC IN ENGLAND. On April 30, England suffered its first civilian casualties when a German mine-laying bomber was shot down and crashed into the garden of a house at Clacton, Essex. After tearing its way through several houses, it exploded. Two persons in addition to the crew of the bomber were killed, and 160 injured. The top photograph conveys some idea of the extent of the damage. The mass of twisted metal on the left is one of the engines of the bomber, while on the right is seen all that was left of the plane itself.

British warships run the gantlet of Nazi bombers off Norway

BRITISH FLEET PLAYS ITS PART IN THE EVACUATION OF NORWAY. The successful evacuation of the Allied forces from Namsos and Aandalsnes early in May was in large measure due to the brilliant work of the Royal Navy. Approaching close to the coast, they put up a covering fire with their heavy guns and helped to keep the enemy in check while the troops were taken off. These pictures show an attack on a British aircraft carrier. Top right, a salvo of bombs is seen exploding just in front of an aircraft carrier. Bottom right, is a view from the deck of one of the escort ships. Bottom left, is a photo of the explosions, taken from the deck of the aircraft carrier. Top left, anti-aircraft pom-poms going into action against the German planes.

INVASION FROM THE SKIES. Shortly after 4 a.m., on Friday, May 10, the peace of Holland's countryside was broken by the drone of aircraft and the skies were filled with white objects floating earthwards, the vanguard of Germany's army of paratroops. With machine guns, portable radio transmitters and even folding bicycles, they descended on Holland and established themselves in fields, behind dykes and in empty houses. One detachment seized the airfield at Rotterdam, while others landed at Delft, four miles south of The Hague, and tried to cut off the Dutch capital. Throughout the day parachutists continued to land at

strategic points all over the country, and although they suffered severe casualties, many detachments succeeded in holding vital points and paving the way for further landings of men from troop-carrying planes. Numbers of paratroops are believed to have landed wearing Dutch uniforms or disguised as civilians and even women. The pictures show (top left) paratroops being launched from a plane. Bottom left, their approach over the roof tops as they prepare to land in a Dutch village. In the above picture a number of paratroops have just made a landing, the man in the back is "spilling" air from his chute.

R.A.F. RAID ON WAALHAVEN. This airfield was one of the first German objectives in Holland, and here the Nazis consolidated their position as Dutch artillery and the R.A.F. launched a furious attack. For six hours waves of planes dropped their bombs with deadly accuracy. Direct hits were scored on the hangars and the ground defenses were reduced to impotence. The damage rendered the airfield unusable for a considerable period after the attack. The picture shows demolished hangars and other damage to the airfield.

AFTER GERMAN BOMBING. In spite of his oft-repeated declaration that he would never wage war against innocent women and children, Hitler sent his planes against many towns in France, Belgium and Holland on the first day of his drive through the Low Countries. Amsterdam was one of the cities visited by the Nazi bombers and much damage was done to life and limb as well as to property. The picture above shows a grief-stricken father, himself wounded, gazing outside his home at the body of his young daughter.

GRAND DUCHY OVERRUN. This little country, sandwiched between France, Belgium and Germany, was the next stop on the Nazi time-table on that eventful May 10. With only a nominal army of some 250 men, this little state could do no more than raise an ineffectual protest. The picture shows German armed motor cyclists crossing into Luxemburg to meet the French troops which had gone to the aid of the Grand Duchy.

INVASION OF BELGIUM. In addition to their thrusts into Holland and Luxemburg, the Germans crossed the Belgian frontier at four points on the morning of May 10. By demolishing bridges and rail lines, the Belgians managed to slow the enemy advance the first day. The pictures show (top) Nazi railroad repair men checking the railroad for sabotage and (below) troops and equipment being ferried across a river.

AID FOR A STRICKEN FRIEND. As soon as the news of Germany's violation of Dutch and Belgian neutrality became known the British and French governments took steps to aid these two countries. In the picture at top is a French tank passing a procession of farm carts loaded with child refugees and at the bottom Belgian townsfolk welcoming a British armored car on the first day of the Nazi invasion.

THE ALLIES RETURN TO BELGIUM. After twenty-six years British and French troops returned to the aid of Belgium and within a few hours of the invasion crack troops of the Allies were across the border. In the picture, at top, an allied Bren gun detachment is watched by Belgian civilians as it passes through a border town and at the bottom Belgian soldiers are seen with British soldiers who have come to fight beside them.

Belgian civilians flee before the Nazi terror   May 10-11, 1940

DRIVEN FROM THEIR HOMES. The stark tragedy of modern warfare is forcefully illustrated in these pictures of Belgian refugees fleeing before the advancing German armies. The pictures show (top) refugees leaving a shattered town carrying their belongings and below, an aged Belgian couple, fleeing before the invader, take a much needed rest by the roadside.

FLIGHT FROM THE BOMBS. The retreating refugees constituted a grave problem for the defending forces as the roads became so blocked with people and vehicles passing in the opposite direction that it was only with the greatest difficulty that military traffic could make its way to the front. The above picture shows refugees passing through a blazing Belgian village to escape the terror.

THE UMBRELLA FOLDS. Confidence in the government led by Neville Chamberlain was seriously undermined by the general conduct of the war and after a debate on the question in the House of Commons on May 8, Mr. Chamberlain invited members of the Opposition to serve under him in a reconstructed cabinet. Labor, however, refused and on May 10 Mr. Chamberlain resigned and was succeeded by Winston Churchill, seen above outside No. 10 Downing Street, official residence of the Prime Minister, with Brenden Bracken, British Minister of Information, on his way to address a session of Parliament, as a London policeman, equipped with gas mask, stands at the salute.

DISLIKE FOR THE ALLIES. Relations between the Allies and Italy had been strained before and since the outbreak of war, but it was not until May that the Italian press seriously began a campaign of hate against the Allies. The Italian people as a whole had little or no dislike of the Western powers, but amongst the student class officially inspired demonstrations against the Allies broke out in many Italian cities. The picture shows Italian students in Rome giving vent to their hatred for the Allies.

The rubber boat becomes a vital part of modern warfare

GERMANS OVERRUN HOLLAND IN A FIVE-DAY CAMPAIGN. While Nazi paratroops were landing behind the Dutch lines, armored columns were crossing the frontier. By the night of May 10 these had advanced to the Maas, crossed the river and entered Maastricht. The following day they crossed the Albert Canal over a bridge which had not been blown by the defenders. Farther north the enemy crossed the River Yssel, near Arnhem and by May 12 both the Maas and Yssel had been crossed at several points and the Dutch troops were falling back. By the 13th the situation had become so serious that Queen

Wilhelmina and the government sought refuge in England. Meanwhile German forces advancing in North Brabant had captured the Moerdyk Bridge which connects that province with South Holland and armored columns in the very heart of the country established contact with air-borne troops that had landed in the opening days of the campaign. Rotterdam fell, and at 1 a.m., on May 14, the Dutch commander gave up further resistance. The picture shows German troops paddling across the Maas at Maastricht in rubber boats, near a bridge destroyed to impede their advance.

GERMANS PRESS HOME THE ATTACK IN BELGIUM. After crossing the Albert Canal on May 11, the Germans advanced towards Tongres and Waremme. Troops that had crossed the frontier farther north pushed southwards, their objective being the eastern end of the Liége-Louvain-Brussels railway. The Belgian Army which had taken up positions on the Meuse and the Albert Canal was forced to fall back on the second line of defense after making an heroic stand against the German mechanized units. British and French forces were rushing up in support. The top picture shows German soldiers making a dash across exposed railroad tracks. Below are German tanks advancing through a small town along the shallow bed of a canal—an easier way to travel than the congested and damaged roads of Belgium.

DRIVE TOWARDS THE FRANCO-BELGIUM FRONTIER. While the Belgian fortress at Liége still held out, the German attack south-west of the city pressed forward towards Brussels and the real and ultimate objective, Northern France. This attack was slowed down by the fierce resistance of the Belgian troops, and the perpetual harassing of the advancing German columns by the Royal Air Force. Where the Belgian troops were forced to fall back, they destroyed bridges and means of communication. The picture shows a German light tank checked by a river, the bridge across which has been blown up.

Brussels in flames after air bombardment by the Nazis

BELGIUM'S CAPITAL FEELS THE NAZI WRATH. On May 15 the German high command announced that it no longer regarded Brussels, historic capital of Belgium, as an open city. It stated that air reconnaissance had established beyond doubt that military columns were moving through the city, and that the German Air Force intended, therefore, to attack all military objectives. Even before this, and until the fall of the city

on May 17, Brussels was subjected to repeated and destructive German air attacks both with high explosive and incendiary bombs. The worst raid took place on Sunday, May 12, when waves of German bombers destroyed many of the buildings on the outskirts of the city. The picture shows firemen dealing with the effects of a bomb which had exploded and wrecked shops and dwelling houses on one of the main streets.

Holland capitulates as Rotterdam is ruthlessly bombed

THE AGONY OF ROTTERDAM. Holland's decision to lay down her arms on May 14 followed the appalling German air attack on that day on her second greatest city. For three hours Rotterdam, without anti-aircraft defenses, was continuously and ruthlessly bombed. An area of two square miles in the heart of the city (the large white patch in centre of the aerial photograph on the right) was completely devastated, killing 30,000 persons. As the bombing ceased, vast fires followed, and hundreds of terrified women and children who

had sought refuge in shelters were drowned by the water from broken water mains. On the left the city at peace is seen from the air: to the right of the main street, the Coolsingel, rises the tower of the Town Hall, with the Post Office in the foreground. After the bombardment (right) the line of the street could hardly be traced; the Town Hall was a complete wreck, and the Stock Exchange a heap of rubble. Two hospitals in the heart of the city were destroyed as this great city felt the Nazi wrath.

Blitzkrieg—The German advance moves ever southwards

TIDES OF WAR SWEEP ON. The "bulge," that master-stroke of German strategy, resisting all the Allies' attempts to close it, or to cut the vanguard's communications with their bases, steadily widened and deepened, and the German advance swept like a flood into Northern France. Bombarding every obstacle, they thundered on, reducing towns, villages and farmhouses to flaming ruins. Reaching the Meuse from Liége

to Namur on May 14, their colossal concentration of tanks and aircraft pressed southward and westward, until, after the Belgian surrender on May 28, the tide had engulfed all Holland, Belgium and France north of the Somme. Above, German soldiers, their bayoneted rifles at the carry, advance cautiously over the scorching streets of a burning town, preparing to deal with any enemy snipers lurking among the ruins.

TOMMY ATKINS IN BELGIUM. One obvious result of the first stages of the "bulge" was added pressure on Louvain and Liége. The former was held by the B.E.F. who resisted stubbornly. Louvain's famous library, destroyed during the first World War, was again severely damaged. The picture above shows an anti-tank gun emplaced at a strategic point amidst houses which have been shattered by bombardment.

FAREWELL TO HOME. On May 15 the B.E.F. evacuated Louvain, which was subjected to terrific shell fire. The picture above is only one of hundreds of similar scenes as the exhausted refugees hurriedly left their wrecked homes taking with them just what they could snatch of their personal belongings.

FRENCH TANKS IN ACTION. The outstanding feature of the German campaign in Holland and Belgium was their use of mechanized units. Tanks and armored cars, supported by aircraft, led the German attack in all cases. Hurriedly organized defenses were of little avail against this new method of warfare, and the Allies strove to effect a counter blow with similar weapons. On May 14 the first clash between French and German mechanized units was reported, and a few days later a French tank offensive was launched in the Sedan-Rethel area. The top picture shows French tanks crashing through a wood. Below, a French tank is seen standing in a village street near Rethel. In the background can be seen a barrier specially constructed to stop the progress of enemy tanks; it conceals a German motorized column held up by the French.

THE INVADERS HOIST THEIR FLAG. On May 17 Brussels capitulated after it had been blasted and scarred by terrific aerial attacks (see pictures on pages 106-107). Here is seen the Nazi standard being flown over the captured capital. Thus, for the scond time in a quarter of a century, an enemy flag flew triumphantly over the Belgian metropolis. The enemy remained the same—only the symbol of its oppression had altered its design from the eagle to the swastika.

THE FRENCH CALL ON A DISCIPLE OF FOCH. At the height of the battle of the "bulge" the world was astounded by the news that General Maurice Gamelin, commander in chief of the French forces, had been superseded by the seventy-three-year-old General Maxime Weygand. Above, is the man of whom Marshal Foch, whose chief of staff the new Generalissimo had been for nine years, including the darkest days of the German advance of 1918, had said: "When France is in danger, send for Weygand."

ADVANCE OVER THE RIVERS. By May 20 the Germans were approaching Amiens, and farther east advance detachments had reached the Aisne. Fully equipped to deal with all obstacles that might hold up their progress, they crossed the river by pontoon bridges, like that seen above, which could be rapidly erected. The speed with which the enemy succeeded in crossing France's water defenses was largely responsible for the spectacular advances achieved by the Germans during the early stages of the struggle.

THE PANZER DIVISIONS ROLL THROUGH FRANCE. For their rush into Northern France the Germans used vast numbers of monster tanks, in advance of which dive bombers cleared away many ground obstacles. Light armored car and motorcycle units followed to prepare the ground for the infantry. The pictures above show (top) a mixed motorized column passing through a French town which has been heavily bombed, and, below, German reinforcements crossing into France past a French customs post.

A DAY OF DISASTER FOR ALLIED HOPES. The Germans, capturing Amiens, Arras and Abbeville, reached the sea on May 21, despite most desperate resistance by the Allies. On that day, too, was announced the capture of General Henri Honoré Giraud, commander of the French Ninth Army, at Sedan. Above, he is seen arriving, a prisoner, at a German airport. General Giraud escaped and rejoined the French command early in 1942. Below, B.E.F. troops are following up a bombing attack though a wood.

DESTRUCTION FROM THE AIR. Picture at the top shows an open town in Northern France as the Nazi raiders left it, the wrecked shop facade in the foreground still advertising funeral furnishings; bottom, the main street in another town, one end of which has been reduced to a heap of fallen masonry.

HOSPITALS AND CHURCHES FAIL TO ESCAPE. Picture at the top shows a ward in a French hospital from which the patients, unprotected even by the Red Cross, have been removed to safer quarters, while below, picture shows the altar steps of a village church covered with debris from the shattered superstructure.

YORKSHIRE AND EAST ANGLIA HIT. When on May 25, for the first time since 1918, German bombs fell on English towns in Yorkshire and Essex, the long-awaited air attack found Britain well prepared. Only eight civilians were injured and material damage was slight. Above, the guns of an east coast anti-aircraft battery are displaying the deadly accuracy of their aim by the even spacing of their bursts of shell fire; below, residents of a Yorkshire town are clearing away the debris caused by a bomb explosion.

BRITISH AT MENIN GATE. In the last days of May the B.E.F., still assisted by the Belgian armies, held in bulldog grip the plains of Western Flanders behind Dunkirk, while the bulge on their right flank widened and the onrushing German mechanized columns moved to surround them and cut them off from the sea. Some of the fiercest fighting took place at Ypres, round the Menin Gate (seen above), the memorial to the British troops who fought and fell in the defense of Belgium during the First World War of 1914–18.

ALLIES CAPTURE NARVIK. Although the Allied forces had withdrawn from Central Norway, the attack on Narvik continued. By May 25 the Allies were twelve miles away, and the main German force, withdrawing to Bjornfjell, left only 250 men to defend the town, which on the 28th fell to a joint British-Norwegian force. Above, French troops are crossing a railway cutting near Narvik; at the village of Bjervik, seen below in flames, landed part of the Allied force which eventually captured the town.

KING LEOPOLD ORDERS "CEASE FIRE." The bitterest blow the Allied cause had yet suffered came on May 28, when the Belgian King ordered his troops to cease fire, leaving the Allied left wing undefended. His order, repudiated by his Cabinet as unconstitutional, was obeyed by the bulk of his troops. Above, the King, with his War Minister, General Denys, is seen, just after his surrender; below, Belgian infantry, on the last day of their participation in the struggle, are running to take shelter from an air bombardment.

AFTER TWENTY-FIVE YEARS. A company of German cyclists enter the capital during the occupation of Belgium. Despite King Leopold's surrender on May 28, the Belgian Cabinet and Parliament refused to accept the King's decision and Belgian soldiers continued to fight until the whole of the country was occupied early in June, bringing back memories of the days of 1914–18,

RED CROSS EMBLEM BOMBED. A damaged Red Cross train after it had been attacked by German aircraft in the northern part of France as the Allies were pushed back to the Channel. This was only one of the many incidents of the ruthless Nazi violations of the Geneva Convention during the German drive across the continent.

THE CHIMNEY SWEEPS LOOK ON. Clad in their traditional garb, top hats perched on their heads, these Sweeps get off their bicycles to survey the incoming Nazi troops in a Danish town. It was a rare sight for the Nazi invaders to find any people on the streets of the towns which they occupied on this mad plunge.

CAUTIOUS INVADERS. German shock-troops enter a deserted village with their eyes peeled for snipers or even any civilians crossing their path in this village, which like many others had been abandoned.

"ARTILLERY FIRE ON BOTH SIDES." The familiar words of the French official communique are here illustrated from the Nazi side of the front as their heavy railroad gun is shown in action on the Western front.

A PILL BOX FALLS ON THE MAGINOT LINE. A Nazi soldier photographed in the act of throwing a hand grenade through a gun opening of a French pill box near the Maginot Line.

The R.A.F. tries to turn the tide of battle in France

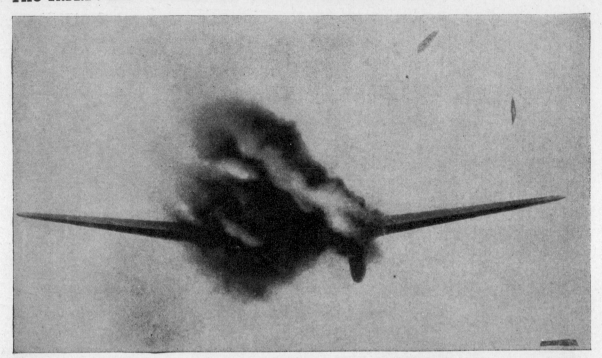

MORE THAN "GROUND STRAFING." The R.A.F. made magnificent efforts to impede the Nazi attack on Northern France. By day and night ceaseless waves of "Wellington," "Hampden" and "Blenheim" bombers, eluding the enemy defenses, went on to rain destruction on German communications behind the lines in the Rhineland and Holland, while more than 1,500 enemy planes were brought down between the invasion of Belgium and the last week in May. One British squadron of twelve fighters shot down at least thirty-seven enemy planes in a single day, May 29, while other squadrons dropped water and ammunition for the use

GERMAN TRANSPORT

ROAD

INCENDIARY BOMBS FALLING FROM PLANE

of the garrison of British and French troops and marines who were heroically holding Calais against terrific German pressure during the Dunkirk evacuation. Meanwhile, as the Nazi troops moved, their mechanized columns and supply trains were riddled with machine gun fire from the air. Top left, a Heinkel, its engines and tanks ablaze, is about to crash in a heap of flaming wreckage. Bottom left, a low-flying plane secures a photo of the enemy horse transport column it is attacking. Right, Fairey "Battle" planes are ground strafing German motorized units with a salvo of incendiary bombs along a French highway.

131

Map of the German advance through Belgium and France

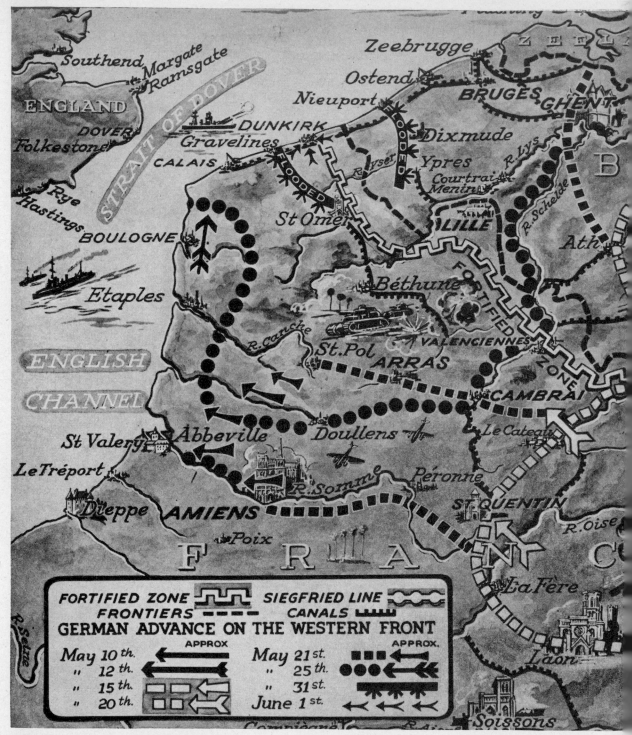

GERMAN ADVANCE FROM MAY 10 TO JUNE 1. Germany's brilliant plan of campaign in Northern France and Belgium consisted of a wide sweep through the Low Countries, to draw the Allied armies northwards, followed by a swift thrust against the French right flank near Sedan, and an advance towards the coast to cut the Allied armies in two and encircle their left wing. The French were taken completely by surprise when the Germans on May 14 hurled their armored divisions against the comparatively lightly

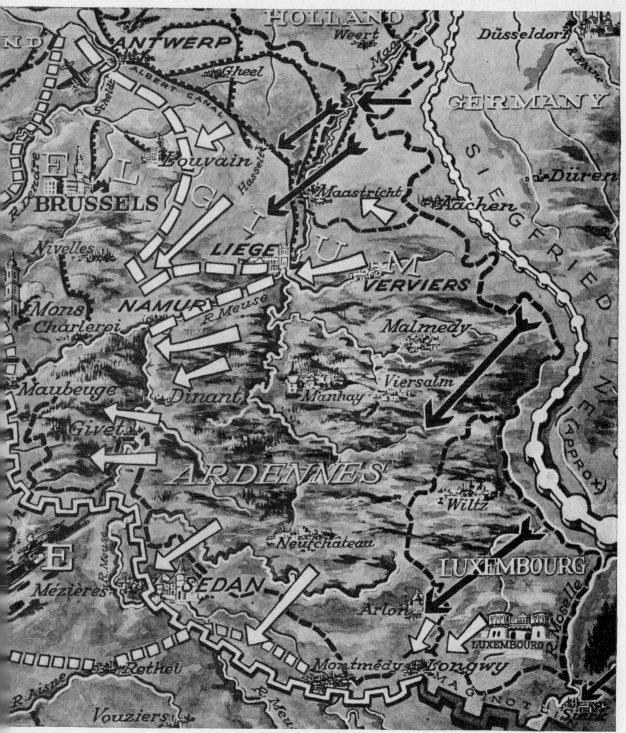

held defenses near Sedan, and drove a rapidly enlarged bulge into the French lines. After Boulogne had
fallen on May 23 the Germans violently attacked the Belgian left flank, and Belgium surrendered on May 28,
leaving the British front unsupported. The Allies fell back towards Dunkirk, whence they were evacuated
by sea, and Belgium, Holland and all France north of the Somme were thus now in German hands. The
arrows indicate the spearheads of the enemy attack; the lines show the positions reached by the German
advanced troops on various dates.

Dunkirk: The beginning of one of history's great stories

MARCH TO DUNKIRK. The laying down of their arms by the Belgians left the B.E.F. in Belgium and N.W. France in imminent danger of being surrounded and driven into the sea, for on May 23 and 24 the Germans had reached the channel at Boulogne and Calais. An attempt to break through to the south to join the French being hopeless, it was decided to fight a rearguard action and attempt withdrawal by sea. Harassed

on every side and from the skies by the Nazis, the weary British soldiers, many of them after a continuous fighting march from the Luxemburg border, fell back towards Dunkirk, to start what the British Admiralty called "The most extensive and difficult combined operation in British naval history." Above, a contingent of them are seen marching into the town, which shows many signs of the heavy bombardment.

Dunkirk: The B. E. F. awaiting evacuation from the beach

HOMEWARD BOUND. On May 30 the world heard that one of the most amazing military operations of all time was in progress. Many of the British troops had reached Dunkirk and were already being evacuated under fire of hundreds of German bombers, by a flotilla of 887 ships of every size and shape. The first men arrived in England on May 30, the last on June 3, more than 330,000 in all reaching safety. In the upper picture, taken from a destroyer, troops are seen on the sands at Bray Dunes wading out waist-deep

to meet the little boats, two of which can be seen in the foreground, that will convey them to the rescuing ships. Below, troops are drawn up on a beach awaiting the strange gathering to take them to safety. During the entire time of their long wait for rescue, the men were subjected to almost continuous bomb and machine gun attacks from German planes, which might have been considerably more serious than they were had it not been for British fighters and anti-aircraft batteries which engaged the enemy raiders.

137

Dunkirk: The ships that saved the wounded May 27-June 3, 1940

BOUND FOR BLIGHTY. Among the evacuees from Dunkirk were a number of wounded, both British and French, from the armies that had fought in the Battle of Flanders. These were, as far as possible, convoyed in ships painted white and marked with a Red Cross, but this did not relieve them from the attentions of the Nazi bombers. Above, a hospital ship is taking off wounded from a narrow jetty; below, a destroyer setting out with crowded decks for the voyage home to safety.

TROOPS WAIT FOR RESCUE. Waiting their turn to find places in the rescue vessels, the troops at Dunkirk scattered over the neighboring sand dunes, taking such rough cover as they could find from the Nazi planes, and going down to the beach in batches as boats became available. This chain of men, neck-deep in water, but many still with their rifles and equipment, is wading out from the shore to scramble up the ship's side and join their buddies who already line the deck.

REARGUARD COVERS THE EMBARKATION. During the evacuation from the sands, thousands of men carried a rearguard action on the outskirts of Dunkirk in order to hold up the advance of the enemy and draw off as far as possible the artillery attacks on the town and the rescue ships. Meanwhile, a small British detachment sent to hold Calais, to reduce German pressure on Dunkirk, held out against enormous odds for several days, thus contributing invaluably to the withdrawal of the main body of the B.E.F.

Practically the whole of this gallant force was either killed or taken prisoner. To the last moment, unprotected even by dug-outs on the open ground, small groups of men armed only with ordinary service rifles did what they could to reply to the incessant bombing and machine gunning of the Nazi planes. Above, one such defender is seen falling to a shrapnel hit, his rifle still defying the enemy in the skies. In the distance bombs aimed at the rescue ships raise huge columns of water as they fall harmlessly into the sea.

THE R.A.F. IN ACTION. The success of the Dunkirk operation was largely due to the work of the R.A.F., who, in the words of Winston Churchill, "decisively defeated the main strength of the German Air Force and inflicted a loss of nearly four to one." The ships were guarded on their channel passage by Lockheed Hudson coastal command planes, one of which is seen above approaching Dunkirk. In the background smoke is rising from oil tanks destroyed by the R.A.F.

DUNKIRK COMMANDERS LEAVE. Largely responsible for the success of the evacuation was Admiral Jean Abrial (above), Commander-in-Chief of the French naval forces at Dunkirk, who was among the last to leave the town, which was occupied by the Germans on June 4. Not until four-fifths of his army was in safety did Lord Gort, British Commander-in-Chief, cross to England. Below, he is being welcomed by a commissionaire outside the War Office, an old comrade-in-arms of the First World War.

DUNKIRK MEN COME HOME. The ships which brought the Dunkirk heroes to safety were constantly attacked by Junkers dive bombers which flew low over them and strafed the crowded decks, but the guns of their naval escorts and the counter-attacks of the R.A.F. fighter planes were so effective that little damage befell them while crossing the channel. Above is a view of two of the destroyers which acted as transports on their arrival at a home port.

TIRED, BUT STILL CHEERFUL. The last men were withdrawn from Dunkirk on the night of June 3-4, leaving the town unusable by the enemy. It had been estimated at the beginning of the operation that 20,000 or 30,000 men might be saved, but although losses were considerable, the total number of allied troops evacuated reached the amazing total of 335,000. Above, some of them are being welcomed with refreshments at a wayside station in England, tired out but still cheerful.

THE ARMADA RETURNS. Many of the boats used in the Dunkirk operation were manned by amateur crews, and came from the Thames and the coast towns of south east England. A Thames boat firm, acting as a clearing house, collected small craft of all kinds, especially motor boats, from London's river. Many were sunk or damaged during the evacuation, but the majority returned, like those seen above as they are being towed up the Thames back to their "peace station" to resume a calmer life as pleasure boats.

REPEAT PERFORMANCE. On June 3, the Royal Navy repeated an exploit of 1918 by sinking two cement-laden blockships (seen in top picture) across the lock entrance to the canal at Zeebrugge, and destroying the sea gates and lock mechanism of the canal. No damage or casualties were suffered during the operation, which was carried out under heavy machine gun fire and bombing from the air. Below, some wounded French soldiers from Dunkirk, practice "thumbs up" on arrival at an English hospital.

PARIS BOMBED FROM THE AIR. The German sweep through France to the south was heralded on June 3 by a severe air raid on Paris during the noon hour. About 300 planes, twenty-five of which were shot down, flying at a height of five miles, dropped indiscriminately more than 1,000 bombs, securing fifteen direct hits on a hospital, killing or wounding thirty children in one of the five schools hit, and inflicting many casualties, including more than 250 deaths. The picture shows firemen searching for victims in the ruins.

FRANCE'S GUNS HIT BACK. The French did all they could to slow down the German advance. While their tanks sought to hold up the Nazi onrush, Allied planes ceaselessly battered the German communications, and the mobile French 75mm. guns, using armor-piercing shells, accounted for many of the enemy's vehicles. Picture at top shows camouflaged French guns pounding the unseen invaders while, below, a heavy caliber gun is directing its fire against an advancing tank column.

R.A.F. OVER GERMANY. Besides maintaining unceasing air attacks on the communications of the advancing Nazis in France, during the first days of June, R.A.F. bombers nightly raided oil depots, factories, and other military objectives in the industrial centres of North Germany, and many Ruhr and Rhineland towns; more than 400 bombs were dropped in one raid on a Frankfort oil depot on June 4. While German anti-aircraft guns, such as those of the battery above, took their toll, the defense proved ineffective.

DRIVE TOWARDS THE FRENCH CAPITAL. On June 5 the Germans opened a furious drive on the Weygand Line. A heavy artillery and tank attack, followed up by half a million infantrymen, covered by dive bombers was thrust from the region of Amiens and Laon towards Compiegne. French anti-tank defenses, hurriedly improvised, though supported by tank and air counter-attacks, could do little or nothing to stem the drive. The picture shows German infantry leaving cover to follow up the advance.

MUSSOLINI'S "STAB IN THE BACK." Italian non-belligerency ceased on June 10, when Benito Mussolini, in a speech in Rome, declared war on Great Britain and France. President Roosevelt hailed the Duce's choice of the blackest hour in France's history as a "stab in the back." In the picture above, Italian troops are marching down the Passo Romano in Rome after Mussolini had concluded his speech.

MUSSOLINI WATCHES HIS WAR BIRDS SOAR. Italy's Duce, in company with staff officers, watching his planes take off on their first bombing raid on French territory. Italy made no immediate spectacular moves, confining herself at first to air warfare on Alexandria, Malta, Gibraltar and French bases within reach. To these the R.A.F. replied with an intensive air campaign in Northern Italy, especially Turin.

Map showing German advances in the battle for the French capital

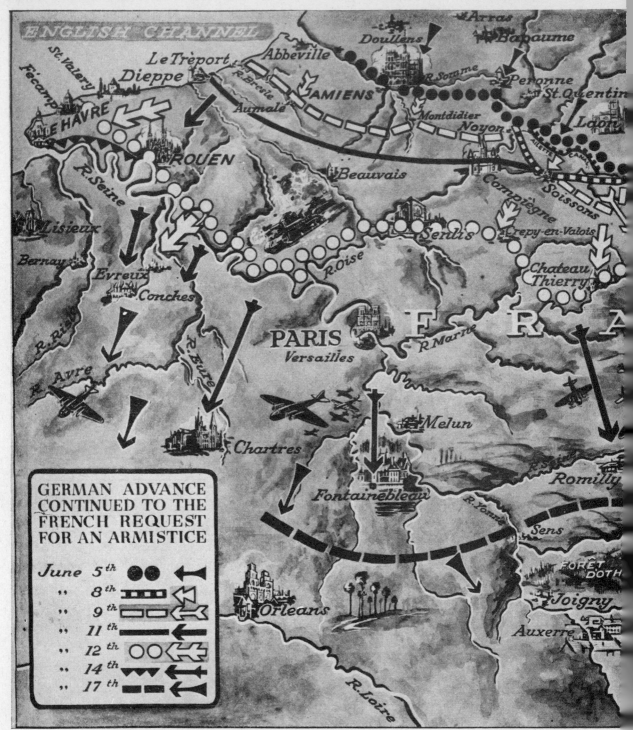

GERMAN ADVANCE CONTINUED TO THE FRENCH REQUEST FOR AN ARMISTICE

June 5th	●● ◀
„ 8th	▭▭▭ ◁
„ 9th	▭ ▭ ⬅
„ 11th	⬅
„ 12th	○ ○ ⬅
„ 14th	▼▼▼ ⬅
„ 17th	▬ ▬ ⬅

THE DRIVE ON PARIS. A slight relaxation of enemy pressure in the first days of June was followed on the 5th by an advance over the Ailette Canal; on the 9th the Germans occupied Soissons By June 11 the battle for the capital was at its peak, the enemy had reached the Seine and were attempting the crossing under a smoke screen, while further east a salient was formed near Chateau-Thierry in an attempt to

encircle the capital. On the 14th Paris fell, the Allies falling back in an attempt to reform their line to the south. On the 15th the Seine was crossed east of Paris near Romilly and German advance guards reached Chaumont, pressed on towards Dijon and entered Verdun on the same day. On the 16th France asked for an armistice but the advance continued until the 22nd. The arrows show the direction of the main thrusts.

THE NAZIS ENTER PARIS. A German heavy motorized unit, passing the Obelisk.

The swastika flies over the French capital

PARIS IN NAZI OCCUPATION. As the Germans took over Paris from the French civil officials, the swastika flag was unfurled on the city's principal buildings, among them the Eiffel Tower, the Hotel de Ville, the Hotel Crillon, where the German staff established its headquarters, and, bitterest of all, the Arc de Triomphe, beneath which lies the tomb of France's unknown soldier of 1918. The picures show: above, German officers, accompanied by a French civil official, looking out over Paris from the top of the Arc de Triomphe, the swastika flag flying before them; below, crowds watching a German animal transport column passing a saluting point in the neighborhood of the Arc de Triomphe.

MORE BRITISH TROOPS TO FRANCE'S AID. When the German onslaught on Paris was at its height, Mr. Churchill promised that all possible help would be sent to support France. On June 15 a reconstructed B.E.F. was ready to sail, among it men who but a fortnight before had escaped from Dunkirk. But with the collapse of France many a transport, like that seen above departing from an English port, its deck crowded with Canadians, was recalled when only a few miles from British shores.

BOUND FOR AMERICA. Events in the Low Countries and France, and the expected blitzkrieg on Britain, caused the American government to urge its nationals to leave the island at once. On June 15 the U.S. liner Washington (above, with tender in foreground bringing passengers from shore) sailed from Galway with about 2,000 U.S. Citizens. On its voyage the ship was stopped by a submarine, and passengers ordered to the boats, but after identification the ship was allowed to proceed unharmed.

FRANCE GIVES UP. Paris had fallen and the collapse of France followed. Premier Paul Reynaud resigned in favor of Marshal Philippe Petain, who immediately asked Germany for an armistice, neglecting Winston Churchill's offer of a Franco-British union of nations. Meanwhile German troops (top) advanced relentlessly south of Paris, reaching the Langres Plateau on the 16th and on the 18th occupying Belfort and Dijon. On the same day Metz fell to the Nazis. Below Adolf Hitler is seen inspecting a captured heavy tank.

DECIDE TERMS OF ARMISTICE. Using the Spanish dictator, General Francisco Franco as mediator, Germany consented to France's request that negotiations should take place for ceasing hostilities, and, in Marshal Petain's words, "concluding an honorable peace." Above, Mussolini and Hitler are seen driving through the streets of Munich on the 17th to their meeting for the settlement of the terms; below, they are cheered by children after their conference. On the 18th the terms were sent to the French government at Bordeaux. On the following day France named her plenipotentiaries for a conference at Compiegne where, twenty-two years before, Marshal Foch had met the Germans on a similar errand.

ANOTHER B.E.F. COMES HOME. The German drive to the west, and France's collapse, made it necessary to bring back the British troops who had been fighting in N.W. France before they could be surrounded. Brought up in camouflaged trucks (above), to Cherbourg and other ports, they marched along the docks (below) to cross the Channel, like the men of Dunkirk, in vessels of every kind, from liners to pleasure craft and tiny steam trawlers. They landed at a port in western England.

HITLER AND MUSSOLINI GLOAT OVER FRANCE. The dictators celebrated the fall of France with triumphal rejoicing. Hitler ordered flags to be flown throughout the Reich for ten days, and church bells to be rung daily for a week. In Paris, German troops with cameras and guide books wandered about sightseeing. Above, with Goering, followed by German staff officers, Hitler is viewing a captured portion of the Maginot Line; below, Mussolini stands in a camouflaged car, touring the battlefront in South East France.

Compiegne: The stage is set for the humiliation of France

END OF THE THIRD REPUBLIC. By Hitler's express orders the stage set for the signing of the Franco-German armistice was exactly the same as on November 11, 1918, when Foch met the German plenipotentiaries on a similar errand. Then the armistice had been signed in a railway coach in the forest of Compiegne. Since 1918 that historic coach had been kept in the Invalides in Paris whence it had been moved after the Treaty of Versailles. Hitler ordered it to be taken to the exact spot in the forest where the act that marked the cessation of hostilities in 1918 had taken place. Hitler could not have conceived a plan more hurtful to the French pride than this resetting of the scene of her earlier triumph. These

scenes of the historic meeting show, top right, the coach being moved up into the exact position it occupied in 1918; top left, a German guard of honor marches round it and the memorial to Germany's 1918 defeat, seen in the left of the picture; bottom left, the French delegates (left to right): General Huntziger, Admiral Le Luc and General Bergeret, followed by M. Leon Noel, in civilian dress, and accompanied by German officials, arrive for the ceremony of the signature; bottom right, Hitler, with General von Brauchitsch and Admiral Raeder on his right and Hermann Goering on his left, followed by Foreign Minister Ribbentrop and Rudolph Hess, leaving the scene. Afterwards the coach was removed to Berlin.

Map showing the severe terms of Nazi armistice June 21, 1940

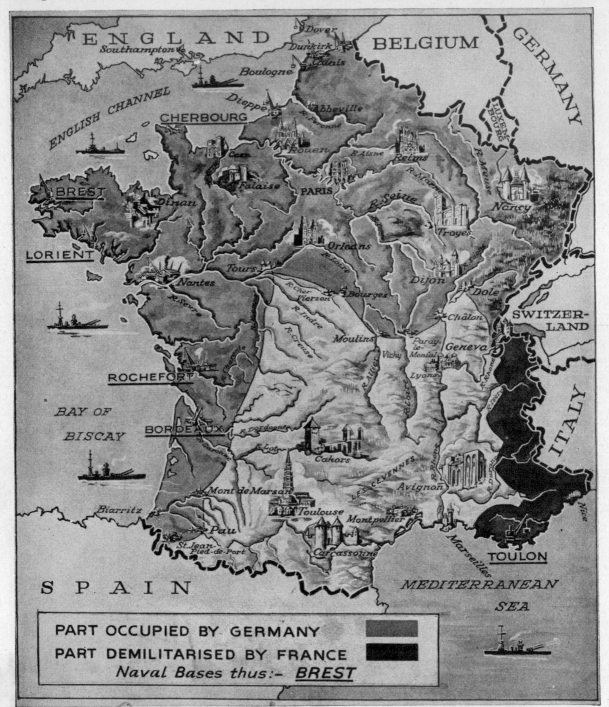

PART OCCUPIED BY GERMANY
PART DEMILITARISED BY FRANCE
Naval Bases thus:- **BREST**

GERMANY OCCUPIES HALF FRANCE. The map shows the full extent of French humiliation under the very severe terms of Germany's Armistice. All North and West France (tinted grey above), her richest provinces, including Paris itself and the whole Channel and Atlantic coastline with its naval bases, were to be occupied at French cost by Germany till the end of the war, while a wide strip (black) along her Italian frontier was demilitarized; all French forces in these areas were to lay down their arms before removal to the unoccupied area for demobilization; French administration might be carried on from any selected town in France, or, by arrangement with Germany, from Paris; for the time being the French chose Vichy.

FRENCH SOLDIERS ESCAPE INTO SWITZERLAND. During the Armistice negotiations the enemy advance went on. On June 17 the Germans announced that the French in Alsace and Lorraine had been surrounded; on the 19th Toul and Luneville were taken. On the 20th, France's third largest city, Lyons, was occupied. As the Germans approached the Swiss frontier, some 50,000 French and Polish soldiers crossed into neutral territory; (above) a Swiss officer watches men crossing the border in a village partly Swiss, partly French, where Swiss soldiers (below) pile the arms taken as they march off for internment.

A PLEDGE OF ASSISTANCE FROM DOWN UNDER. The redoubled determination of every unit of the British Commonwealth to hold on until a final blow had been dealt to Nazi aspirations was emphasized anew as the German attack became wholly concentrated on Britain. Above, Australian ex-service men pledge allegiance to the war effort before the Cenotaph in Sydney. Below, Australia's Parliament debating National Emergency Bill by which the country's resources were placed at government's disposal,

BRITISH NAVY FIRES BREST. French troops aboard a British warship bound for England to continue the fight against the Nazis are shown (top) watching warehouses in the Harbor at Brest go up in smoke; while, bottom, fires blaze among the debris of shattered harbor buildings, made useless by demolition crews of the British Navy in a surprise attack.

A British trawler captures an Italian submarine in Il Duce's waters

BRITISH SUPREMACY IN MEDITERRANEAN. Italy's efforts to establish naval supremacy in Near Eastern waters were not marked by very conspicuous success. The capture of a submarine by any surface vessel is an almost unheard-of event in naval warfare; but on June 22 it was announced that the large Italian submarine Galileo Galilei, captured by the British trawler Moonstone, had been brought into harbor as a prize. On sighting the enemy's periscope Moonstone brought her to the surface with depth charges and re-

plied to her fire with her four-inch gun, four shells from which were enough to induce her to surrender. Above, Moonstone is towing her prize into Aden Harbor. Below are two other aspects of war in the Mediterranean: right, Italian planes dropping salvos of bombs at a British warship in what Italy prematurely called "our sea" demonstrate their bad marksmanship; left, another British warship, unable to find Il Duce's bashful navy, finds time to enjoy a little quiet gunnery practice.

The end of Italy's short campaign against France

FRANCE ACCEPTS ITALIAN TERMS. At the Villa Inchesa, near Rome, on June 24, France received Italy's armistice terms. Signed at 6:15 p.m. that day, they came into force, simultaneously with those of the Franco-German armistice, at 12:35 a.m. on June 25, while Italians troops were still advancing on the Alpine front and had just occupied Mentone. They included demilitarization of zones in France, Tunis, Algeria and Somali-land; full rights for Italy over Jibuti and its railway; demilitarization of the French fleet, and the naval bases at Toulon, Oran, Bizerte and Ajaccio; control of all French airports, and the right to demand the surrender of all or part of the French arms which had been facing Italian forces. All Italian prisoners of war and internees

in French hands were to be handed over to Italy; free transport of goods was to be permitted between Italy and Germany through unoccupied French territory. Italy might demand that French ships should be used for minesweeping, but declared that she did not intend to use units of the French fleet for her own purposes during the war or to lay claim to it on the conclusion of peace. The Italian delegates were Marshal Badoglio (standing), Count Ciano (to his left), Admiral Cavagnari, Generals Pricolo and Roatta, representing the Italian Navy, Air Force and Army; the French were represented by (left to right above) Vice-Admiral Le Luc, M. Leon Noel, and the Generals Huntziger, Parisot and Bergeret.

ANZACS ARRIVE IN ENGLAND. Towards the end of June the first considerable contingent of troops from Australia and New Zealand landed in the Old Country to prepare for active service by a period of intensive training. In the above picture some "diggers" on a few days' leave in London are shown arriving at their social headquarters, the Strand Theatre, Aldwych.

ROYAL WELCOME. Queen Elizabeth, surrounded by officers and men of the navies, armies and air forces of all the Dominions, poses for a picture at the Victoria League Club in London, while, below, a contingent of Australians sets out from their training camp, headed by their band and drum major for a route march.

Britain prepares to meet the foe in the Middle East

THE WATCH IN THE DESERT. The Italian declaration of war had been long expected, and from the beginning of the war full measures had been taken by Britain to protect Egypt and the Suez Canal against Italian attacks. Egypt did not herself undertake hostile action, though she stood ready to defend her territory, warning Italy that any attempt on Cairo would involve her entry into the war by Britain's side. The Red Sea coasts and the desert were ceaselessly guarded by British troops aided by New Zealand,

Indian and Maltese contingents; and the Nile was continuously patrolled by armed motor launches. The pictures show: top left, Arab soldiers holding look-out posts to guard against surprise landings by troops from Italy's African possessions on the Red Sea coast; bottom left, Egyptian soldiers in a sandbagged post guarding a bridgehead in Cairo; top right, men of an English county regiment at Bren gun practice over the sands; bottom right, British tanks and their crews in Cairo awaiting orders to move off into the desert.

TARGETS OF THE NAZI BOMBERS. After the capitulation of France the German Air Force, no longer confining itself to coastal operations, greatly intensified its attacks on Britain, and from June 18 onwards numbers of enemy planes crossed the coast almost nightly. But the people of England were completely unmoved by these attacks. Material damage and casualties were surprisingly small, and R.A.F. fighters and anti-aircraft guns disposed of a heavy percentage of the attackers. In the first week of regular raiding

at least twelve bombers were shot down, and a number more accounted for by anti-aircraft guns—an indication of the amazing response that would be made to bigger attempts to come. The south coast village church (left), set on fire by incendiary bombs, in one of the first raids of the series is receiving attention from the local A.F.S.; while in the picture above is shown all that remains of a London apartment house after a Nazi raid at night in which numerous persons lost their lives as they were trapped in the debris.

DESTRUCTION FROM THE AIR. Many of the bombs dropped by Marshal Goering's Air Force fell on residential areas and caused destruction and misery in the homes of peaceful working-class districts. What is left of a row of houses is seen in the lower picture, while above, one of the victims is removing some of his personal belongings from his Anderson shelter in the yard of his home.

WINGED. Despite the speeding up of the attack from the skies, material damage and casualties were surprisingly small, and R.A.F. fighters and anti-aircraft guns disposed of a heavy percentage of the attackers. The heavy toll paid by the Nazi raiders is shown by the bombers which have been brought down in the sea (top), and in a garden in Southern England (below).

Britain's defense against the raiders

HOW ENGLAND FOUGHT THE BLITZ. The type of defense used against the raiders proved itself again and again. Bombers were repeatedly engaged by fighter aircraft and shot down, or were destroyed in the anti-aircraft barrage. Fighter pilots, constantly on the alert for raiders, are seen running to their planes

on receipt of an alarm (top left). Searchlights (bottom left) pick out the raiders and hold them in their beams while A.A. guns (bottom right) or fighter pilots engage them. The balloon barrage (top right) which effectively prevents dive bombers from approaching their target, brought several raiders down.

CIVILIAN DEFENDERS OF BRITAIN. The work of Britain's airmen and anti-aircraft gunners was matched by all branches of the civil defense services. The Volunteer Observer Corps (above) rendered valuable service in detecting the approach of enemy aircraft, while the Auxiliary Fire Service (below) dealt with fires caused by high explosive or incendiary bombs.

GERMAN TANKER SUNK. In spite of the loss of the French Channel ports, the British Navy and Air Force retained mastery of the English Channel and the Strait of Dover, through which convoy after convoy passed safely, bringing munitions and food supplies to English ports. In this picture, which is taken from an R.A.F. bomber, another plane of the squadron is shown flying above an enemy tanker bombed off the French coast and sinking in a mass of smoke and flames.

LEADERS OF THE FRENCH FORCES. Under the leadership of General Charles de Gaulle, left, a rapidly growing army of free Frenchmen was enrolled in England to fight side by side with the British Army. Admiral Muselier, right, who escaped from France in a destroyer was appointed commander-in-chief of the Free French Navy. A number of vessels manned entirely by French officers and men took part immediately in successful operations.

READY TO CARRY ON. The army of Free Frenchmen was not the only ally saved from the war in France. As soon as it became evident that France had decided to seek an armistice, large numbers of Polish soldiers were quickly transferred to England. They are seen here disembarking from a transport, resolved to prove, in the words of M. J. Mikolajczyk, vice president of the national council of the Polish Republic, "the will and determination to persevere in this struggle for the liberation of Poland."

REFUGEES ARRIVE AS PRISONERS LEAVE. The decision to demilitarize the Channel Islands produced many poignant scenes such as that pictured above, as whole families with what luggage they could carry sought safety in England. At the same time German prisoners of war, who are seen below marching to their embarkation station, were being sent for greater security to internment camps set up in Canada.

THE ARANDORA STAR TORPEDOED. On July 3 news was received that the Arandora Star, carrying 1,500 German and Italian internees to Canada, had been torpedoed and sunk by a German submarine. Many lost their lives through panic, in spite of heroic efforts by their British guards. Above, the liner is seen in peace time, while below, are some of the survivors being landed at a Scottish port.

The British Navy seizes the French fleet

THE TRICOLOR COMES DOWN, THE UNION JACK GOES UP. When France laid down her arms, Britain asked the Petain government to allow the French fleet, lest it fall into German hands, to sail for British ports before Armistice negotiations were completed. But the Armistice, as signed, provided that France's Navy should fall under German control and fast action had to be taken to prevent these ships

being used by the Nazis. On July 3, two battleships, two light cruisers, many destroyers, and nearly 200 smaller craft, including the world's largest submarine, the Surcouf, were taken over, almost without re- sistance, by the British. Above are seen some of the warships that were seized in British ports, eventually to be manned by sailors of the Free French and Allied navies.

ACTION IN ALGERIA. At Oran lay two French battleships, the Dunkerque and the Strasbourg, with many other units of the French fleet. After unsuccessful parleys with Admiral Gensoul, the French officer in command, it became necessary for vice-admiral Sir James Somerville to open fire. Several ships were sunk or damaged in the engagement, the Dunkerque (above) being driven aground and later rendered useless by air bombardment. Below is a general view of the harbor at Oran, where the action took place.

TRIUMPHANT RETURN. On July 6, Adolf Hitler returned to Berlin after eight weeks spent with the army in the field. Ordered by Reich minister Goebbels to give the Fuehrer a welcome "such as Berlin had never seen before," to celebrate the victory in France, large crowds were dragooned to cheer him on his progress through the city, accompanied by his usual squads of storm troopers and S.S. guards. Above, Hitler can be seen standing in the leading car to receive the "mechanized" welcome.

END OF THE THIRD REPUBLIC. On July 9, the French Chamber of Deputies at Vichy voted for the reform of the constitution by 395 votes to 3. Later the Senate confirmed this decision, paving the way for the overthrow of the Republic and for the welding of another dictatorship from the battered fragments of the Constitution. Above, the French National Assembly is seen in session when the Democratic parliament voted itself out of existence. Below, Pierre Laval, vice-premier, is shown on his way to the meeting.

APPEAL FOR ALUMINUM. On July 9 Lord Beaverbrook, Minister of Aircraft Production, made an appeal to the women of England to give up their aluminum pots and pans to help the national effort to build fighter planes. "We want aluminum, and we want it now," said Lord Beaverbrook, for with the collapse of France a valuable source of aluminum had passed into enemy hands. The wonderful response can be judged from the lower picture. Above, is a part of one of the aircraft factories which reaped the benefit.

THE ITALIAN FLEET COMES OUT. The first major action between the British and Italian fleets took place in the Mediterranean on July 9. The enemy squadron, comprising two battleships and a number of cruisers and destroyers, put up a smoke screen as soon as the British appeared and turned tail for home. Later the Italian news agency announced that their navy had fought a "glorious and successful action" with the British Navy. The pictures show (top) shells from the British squadron bursting near an Italian battleship, which is firing dead astern. Below, the guns of an Italian warship in action during the engagement.

FRENCHMEN MARK BASTILLE DAY. July 14, the anniversary of the fall of the Bastille in 1789, is normally a day of national celebration in France. This year the crowds were sombre and dejected, as shown in the picture above of Bordeaux citizens standing in silence before the memorial to those killed in the first world war. Below, General De Gaulle is reviewing a unit of his forces after placing a wreath on the Cenotaph, in London, England's tribute to her dead of the first world war.

German dive bombers attack a convoy in the Channel

AIR BATTLE OVER THE STRAIT OF DOVER.
One of the most determined attacks by the German
Air Force on British shipping in the Strait of Dover
was carried out on 14 July, when about forty dive
bombers escorted by fighters, took part. Although
at least seven enemy planes were destroyed, the
results of the raid were negligible for, as shown in
the picture, almost all the bombs fell into the sea.

MR. CHURCHILL, IN HIS STIRRING
BROADCAST TO BRITAIN AND THE WORLD
ON JULY 14, 1940:—

"All goes to show that the war will be long and hard. No one can tell where it will spread. One thing is certain—the peoples of Europe will not be ruled for long by the Nazi Gestapo, nor will the world yield itself to Hitler's gospel of hatred and domination. . . .

"Here in this strong city of refuge, which enshrines the title deeds of human progress and is of deep consequence to Christian civilization; here, girt about by the seas and oceans where the Navy reigns, shielded from above by the staunchness and devotion of our airmen, we await undismayed the impending assault. . . .

"But be the ordeal sharp or long, or both, we shall seek no terms, we shall tolerate no parley. We may show mercy—we shall ask none."

ENGLAND PREPARES FOR INVASION. Undaunted by Nazi threats of annihilation, Britain prepared to defend herself against attack by sea or air. Barbed wire entanglements were erected at strategic points, as shown on the left, where Big Ben is silhouetted behind its unaccustomed defense. Signposts were removed from all roads (above) and the streets of London (below) were barricaded and strongly guarded.

England prepares to play host to an unwelcome visitor

LOCAL DEFENSE VOLUNTEERS ON THE JOB. The threat of invasion to England was responsible for the introduction of many stringent precautions. In the picture at top, a temporary barricade has been erected on one of the roads in southern England. These barricades were put in position at night, and manned by defense volunteers. In the picture below, L. D. V.'s are learning to throw "Molotov Cocktails."

THE "COCKTAIL" HAS A KICK. The effect of one of the "Molotov Cocktails" on a dummy tank towed by a car is shown. The bombs, which are bottles partially filled with a mixture of gasoline, paraffin and crude oil, were used by the Russians with much success during the Finnish campaign and were named for V. M. Molotov, the Soviet premier and foreign minister.

BRITAIN ON GUARD. On May 14, Anthony Eden had announced the formation of a Home Guard of Local Defense Volunteers. By the middle of July their number exceeded one million, many of them veterans of the last war determined to defend their country to the last ditch. Here an armed guard of L.D.V.'s is patrolling an important point on Britain's system of railway communications, armed with rifle and bayonet, and wearing their official uniform, proving themselves to be Britain's "first reserves against invasion."

THE HOME GUARD NAVY IN ACTION. The activities of the Local Defense Volunteers were not restricted to the land. The Upper Thames Patrol, the "navy" of the Home Guard, kept watch by day and night on the locks, towpaths, bridges and landing steps of London's riverside. Its smart motor launches, most of which were privately owned and manned by amateur yachtsmen, patrolled altogether 125 miles of the Thames. Above, in a picturesque setting, is seen a flotilla of the patrol, its ships dressed, on its way to be reviewed.

"We shall fight on the beaches. We shall never surrender."

DEFENDERS OF THE ISLAND FORTRESS. Following Winston Churchill's words: "We shall defend our island whatever the cost may be . . ." Britain's people's moat was completed in record time and manned by a mixture of regular army men and local defense volunteers. The picture above shows a unit on tactical exercises on one of England's beaches in preparation for any attack.

AMERICA SENDS THE "TOMMY" GUN. New weapons and defense methods were speedily forthcoming to deal with the threat of invasion. From June the entire output—5,000 per month—of the new American weapon, the "Tommy" sub-machine gun, firing 1,500 rounds a minute from either shoulder or hip, was shipped weekly to England. Above, troops training with the new gun advance to attack. Below, a R. A. S. C. squad, brought up in trucks, searches the heather for parachute troops during tactical exercises in England.

Armored cars and tanks patrol the English countryside

"IRONSIDES" AWAIT THE ENEMY. Among the devices for dealing with the expected invader were the aptly-nicknamed "Ironsides," armored cars of a new type, fitted with Bren guns. Some of the new cars, which can operate in the roughest country, are seen (above) moving off for exercises in an English park.

SURPRISE FOR HITLER. England made sure that, if Hitler was to be Britain's first invader for 900 years, he should find a mechanized army awaiting him, and that tanks, which he had exploited so successfully in Europe, were as powerful a weapon in British hands. Above, light tanks are seen on maneuvers.

BRITAIN'S WOMEN FILL THE BREACH. As men in greater and greater numbers were absorbed into the defense forces, their womenfolk stepped forward, not only to play a magnificent part in the arms factories, to become bus drivers and mailmen, to man the farms and bring in the harvest (above), but even formed an "Amazon Corps," later the Women's Volunteer Defense Corps, who learned rifle drill (below) with sticks and umbrellas to take a share in defending themselves against the awaited invader.

DEFENSE MEASURES IN THE UNITED STATES. Although preoccupied by the coming presidential elections, America showed itself during the months of June and July to be increasingly aware of the German threat to world democracy. Among many measures dictated for home defense was the calling up of volunteers for the army, who are seen at a training camp in the lower picture. Above, Colonel Frank Knox, is shown being sworn in as Secretary of the Navy as President Franklin D. Roosevelt looks on.

R.A.F. HITS AT GERMAN BASES. Night after night the bombers of the R.A.F. went forth on their work of destruction, wreaking havoc in German industrial centres and communication lines. Oil depots, plane factories and air fields were their main objectives. Unlike the German Air Force, they concentrated entirely on military objectives and had orders to bring their bombs back rather than drop them at random on non-military areas. Above, a bombing crew is seen on its return from a night's work over Germany. Below, examining bombs in preparation for a night attack.

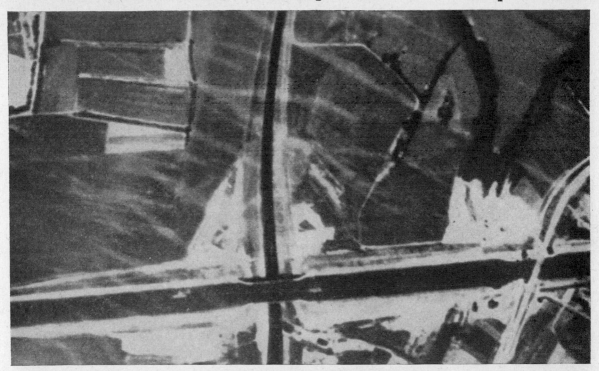

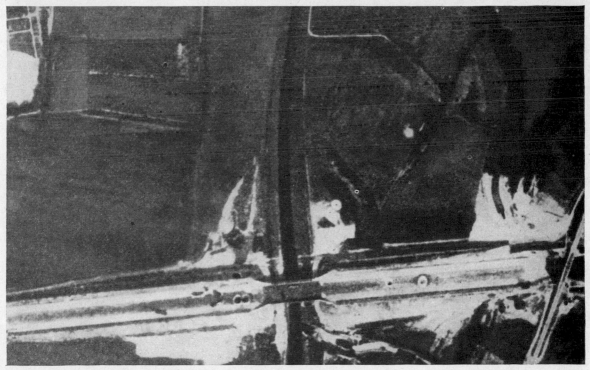

R.A.F. GETS A BULLSEYE. The Dortmund-Ems Canal, an important artery in Germany's waterway system, was singled out as a special objective for the R.A.F., and a resolute attack was made on July 18. Picked crews dropped bombs on the aqueduct carrying the canal over the River Ems. Above, the canal is seen before the raid; barges show white in the black streak (left to right) of the water-filled canal. Below, after the raid, bomb craters in the empty and stranded barges at its sides show the effects of R.A.F. fire.

Death plunge of the Cunard liner Lancastria

VICTIM OF GERMAN DIVE BOMBERS. On July 25 came news of the sinking by Junkers dive bombers of the Cunard White Star liner Lancastria off St. Nazaire, while evacuating British troops from France on June 17. More than half of the 5,000 men on board, mostly British soldiers and airmen, were saved, in spite

of the fact that the ship went under within half an hour of the attack. The above picture, taken from one of the ships that rushed to the rescue shows the sea dotted with men swimming for safety as the liner keeled over preparatory to taking her death plunge.

READY TO FIGHT AGAIN. Throughout the summer of 1940 reconstruction on British soil of foreign units from the occupied countries proceeded apace. On July 21, Great Britain recognized the Czechoslovak government established in London. Above, Dr. Eduard Benes, head of the government, is saluting the colors at a review of Czech troops in southern England. Below, men of the French Foreign Legion, who, after fighting at Narvik escaped to England from Brittany, and joined General De Gaulle, pass in review.

MASS ATTACK ON CHANNEL PORT. On July 29, eighty German planes attempted a surprise raid on shipping in Dover Harbor, the largest air fight up to that date off Britain's coast. Nineteen planes were destroyed by British fighter planes and two by anti-aircraft batteries, against one British plane lost and two damaged. Not a single one of the raiders' bombs fell on land. Above, bursting shells from anti-aircraft batteries are seen in the plane-studded sky as bombs explode in the water, well wide of the vessels at anchor.

Transfer of American destroyers to Britain proposed

AID FOR GREAT BRITAIN. On August 4, General John J. Pershing lent his support in a broadcast to a campaign which had been organized in the United States advocating the sale to Britain of some fifty or sixty of the fleet of decommissioned destroyers, many of them reconditioned, which since the war of 1914–18, had been lying in the Philadelphia Navy Yard, where some of them are seen above. Losses and

the necessity for spreading her fleet over a wide area had placed great demands on the British Navy and the need for more destroyers in convoy duty was urgent. Fifty of the ships were transferred to Britain early in September by a reciprocal agreement in exchange for naval and air bases in British territories in the Atlantic.

POLAND'S NEW ARMY. On August 5 an agreement was signed providing for the reorganization of Poland's armed forces in Britain as a separate unit under the Allied High Command. Above, General Wladyslaw Sikorski, Poland's Premier and Commander-in-Chief, decorates the colors of the Polish Highland Brigade, which fought at Narvik. Below, the British flying boat "Clare," which took off for America when Britain resumed transatlantic air service on August 4, unloading in England after her first round-trip.

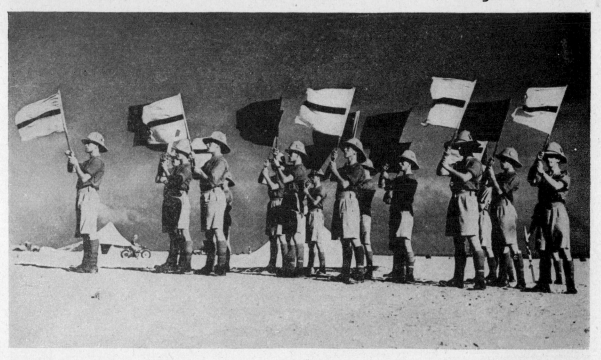

EGYPT AWAITS INVASION. As Italian concentrations were massed for action on the Libyan border in early August, British and Dominion troops in the Western Desert prepared to receive them, dealing destruction meanwhile on Italian planes which raided Alexandria and the inland airfields and desert bases. Above, a British signal corps detachment is seen training in the desert, while below, Egyptian gunners are manning anti-aircraft guns at a coast defense post.

Camels play their part in the defense of British Somaliland

SOMALILAND CAMEL CORPS ON PATROL. On August 4 Italian forces invaded British Somaliland simultaneously from three points. British tactics in this inhospitable and difficult country were directed not to defending every inch of territory, but to harassing the invaders in all possible ways, compelling them to dissipate their forces. Doughty fighters for Britain were the Somaliland Camel Corps shown above now partly mechanized, who put up a stubborn fight before Britain was forced to evacuate on August 19.

PARIS AIRPORT RAIDED. On August 7, the pilot of a British bomber made a lone attack on the German-occupied LeBourget Airfield, outside Paris, where Lindbergh landed at the close of his historic flight in May, 1927. A number of bombs were dropped on the runway where several Nazi planes were standing. Other bombs hit the hangars. The defense was taken by surprise, and the British pilot made a get-away before the Germans had time to get into action. The picture shows Nazi soldiers walking past some of the hangars.

WAR IN THE MEDITERRANEAN. The British Navy and the R. A. F. dealt repeated blows on the Italian fleet while cruising around Mussolini's favorite sea. In one action in Maltese waters a squadron of British light cruisers tackled a detachment of the Italian Navy, including battleships, cruisers and destroyers, damaging a battleship and a cruiser. Above, an Italian ship is seen firing a broadside during the engagement, while the picture below shows the havoc wrought in an enemy battleship by a British shell.

Australian gunners keep their fingers on the trigger

AUSTRALIAN ARTILLERY AT WORK. Further drafts of the Australian Imperial Force arrived in Britain at the beginning of August, including medium and heavy artillery brigades. Above, some of these men from "Down Under" are training with a new tractor 25-pounder medium field gun, easily convertible into an anti-tank gun, with which some of their batteries are equipped. Below, another such gun is being loaded during a field display. Right, some Aussies have discovered that haystacks make good camouflage for howitzers.

FROM THE OLDEST DOMINION. Several artillery units from Newfoundland came to England in the summer of 1940 to take their place alongside of the men from other points of the Empire in the defense of the Homeland. Some of them are seen above manning a howitzer in a park at one of the channel ports. These guns and men were to play a great role in the Battle of Britain, hundreds of Nazi raiders falling to their accurate marksmanship in the unhappy months for England before the German hordes were repelled.

BRITISH READY IN EGYPT. The threatened land attack on Egypt by the Italians in Libya was slow to materialize, water supply difficulties in the Western Desert, over which the Italian troops must cross to reach their objective, dissuading their commanders from hurried action. Meanwhile the British forces defending their country perfected their arrangements for meeting the invader. Above, a R.A.F. bomber formation on patrol over the Pyramids. Below, Egyptian troops in the desert haul a gun into position.

DESTRUCTION IN THE HEART OF LONDON. Through the shattered archway of a damaged building the cameraman obtained this study of modern destruction in the heart of London. Rearing miraculously unharmed amid this smoldering devastation are the twin spires of St. Paul's Cathedral.

PRIME MINISTER IN THE FIELD. In the intervals of organizing the nation's war effort from No. 10 Downing Street, Mr. Churchill made several visits of inspection to defense works, coast fortifications and munitions factories in various parts of the country. Here he is shown, above, being greeted by defense plant workers during a tour of north-east England, and below, inspecting a battalion of the Grenadier Guards.

BRITISH NAVY ATTACKS AFRICAN PORTS. Heavy attacks were made during July and August by the Navy and R.A.F. on Italian ports and supply bases on the Libyan coast, especially Derna, Tobruk and Bardia, the last Italian main forward base for Western Desert operations. Above, an attacking cruiser off the Libyan shore. Below, a gun in action as units of the Mediterranean Fleet bombard a coast port.

A load of bombs for the Axis partners

A WELLINGTON BOMBER LOADS UP. The whole of Western Europe under German and Italian domination was every night the happy hunting ground of British bombing planes, whose operations extended from Norway to Italy, the vast width of the front open to them making it impossible for the enemy to anticipate their next stroke. Above, a train of bombs being loaded into a bomber in preparation for a night's work.

The battle of Britain: Hitler's aerial blitzkrieg begins

MASS RAIDS OVER ENGLAND. The air offensive against Britain started in full force on August 8. From that day until the 19th, when there was a temporary lull, bombers came over almost continuously, attacking airfields, dockyards and munitions works. High explosive and incendiary bombs were released over military and non-military objectives, but the damage done by the raiders, outclassed by the British fighters and harried by the barrage of anti-aircraft fire, was out of all proportion to the losses they sustained. The balloon barrage was singled out in the early raids as a special object of attack. Above, the trail of a barrage balloon shot down by enemy raiders off the S.E. coast. Right (below), another balloon in flames; its attacker can be seen on the right of the picture. Right (above), Nazi raiders scuttle for home as fighters intercept them.

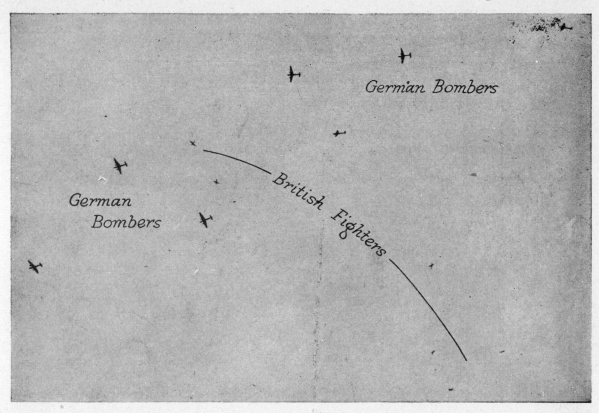

German Bombers

German Bombers

British Fighters

HEAVY COST OF AIR BLITZKRIEG.
The phenomenal successes of the British fighter pilots in their combats with the Nazi raiders were due in large measure to their unbounded faith in their planes. Both the Hurricane and the Spitfire fighters proved themselves time and time again to be faster and more maneuverable than their German counterparts, besides possessing a more powerful and more devastating armament in their eight machine guns. In spite of their best efforts the Messerschmitts escorting the German bombers failed to keep their more nimble opponents at bay or to prevent them from taking a terrible toll of their bomber formations. Above, a Dornier "flying pencil" bomber, its engine aflame, diving to destruction after an encounter with a British fighter. Below, a Nazi airman, whose parachute failed to open when he "bailed out" after the tail of his machine was shot off, crashes on a housetop.

The home guard bags a German bomber   August 18, 1940

DORNIER SHOT DOWN. Not all the spoils of the war over Britain fell to the regulars. On August 18 a detachment of the Home Guard, from their sandbagged emplacement on the outskirts of South London, claimed the first bomber, a Dornier, to fall to the volunteer defenders. They shot it down after 180 rounds of rifle fire. Above are some of the men who shot the bomber down. Below is the result of their lunch-hour labor.

LONDON SCENES AFTER A RAID. Not only hundreds of lives but the furniture and treasures of many homes were saved by the untiring efforts of the rescue workers. Above, a pile of salvaged furniture is waiting in a working-class street to be claimed by its owners. Below, ruined dwelling-houses and shops in the famous South London thoroughfare, Old Kent Road, a short time after one of the heavy raids.

Graveyard of bombers bagged over England   August 8-19, 1940

Planes lost in fighting over Britain and the coast, August 8-19, 1940 (R.A.F. official figures)			
	German planes lost	British planes lost	British pilots safe
August 8	61	18	3
" 9	1	—	—
" 10	1	1	—
" 11	65	26	2
" 12	62	13	1
" 13	78	13	10
" 14	31	7	2
" 15	180	34	17
" 16	75	22	14
" 17	1	—	—
" 18	152	22	8
" 19	4	—	—
TOTAL	711	156	57

WRECKAGE OF THE LUFTWAFFE. The accumulation of scrap material from planes shot down in Britain became such a problem to the authorities that a central dump (above) was established where the useful material was sorted out for conversion in due course into new British planes. On the right, workmen are seen eating their lunch in the wrecked fuselage of a bomber collected from Goering's air armada.

The Germans train their big guns on a Channel convoy

GERMAN SHELLS FAIL TO DAMAGE BRITISH SHIPPING. In early August, German high-velocity guns were massed along the French coast from Calais to Boulogne, which would serve to cover troop transports in an attempt at invading Britain. On the 22nd these guns were brought into action for the first time against a convoy in the Channel, firing a shell a minute for more than an hour as the ships passed through

the narrows—and missing every time. Nazi dive bombers, simultaneously attacking the convoy and its escort from above, were equally unsuccessful, for the skilful seamanship of the British vessels, combined with the accurate fire of the escorting warships, made close approach too hazardous. As the salvos from the German batteries fell harmlessly (above), British destroyers laid smoke screens and dropped smoke floats.

DOVER SHELLED. The cross-channel guns followed up their attack on Channel shipping by bombarding the coast in the neighborhood of Dover for about three-quarters of an hour on the evening of August 22, damaging some buildings, including a church, interior shown above, and causing several casualties.

A shell from France tears up a street in Dover   August 22, 1940

LONG RANGE SHELLING. Members of Dover's civil defense services examining a shell crater in a road close to a church after Nazi long-range guns had spoken from France on August 22. The force of the explosion can be judged by the damage caused to the front of the house on the right of the picture.

NAZI BOMBS FAIL TO WORRY LONDON. If the purpose of the mass raiding was to undermine the Londoner's morale, it was a ludicrous failure. Munitions factories carried on work as bombs fell near them, and in many cases repair work on damaged buildings began within an hour or two of the passing of the Nazi planes. In public shelters men and women played cards or sang, while many thousands, turning over in bed with a word of annoyance as the sirens sounded for another "all-night" raid, settled to sleep again, undisturbed by anti-aircraft fire, until the "raiders passed" signal woke them once more. Above, nuns arrive at a scarred railway station in a bombed suburb to help in rescue work after a raid. Below, the interior of a suburban film house after it had received a direct hit from a Nazi bomb.

NAZI FIGHTER'S LAST FIGHT. The R.A.F. and the anti-aircraft defenses rejoiced in the opportunity given by the August raids to decimate Goering's "invincible" Luftwaffe, and in ten days accounted for 711 Nazi planes (see table on page 239), not bothering to count the probably even greater number so badly mauled that it was unlikely that they could have returned to their bases. The picture above shows one of many German fighters brought down by Hurricanes and Spitfires burning itself out in a field in S.E. England.

Nazi bombers penetrate London's defenses

AIR WAR REACHES THE CAPITAL. On August 16, London was first bombed by Nazi radiers who hit several buildings in the south west suburbs including churches, a hospital and a railway station and opened machine gun fire on people in the streets. London's anti-aircraft guns first came into action on August 18, when delayed action bombs were dropped in the suburbs. It was not until the 25th, however, that the raiders suc-

ceeded in penetrating the outer defenses and reaching the City, that portion of London north of the Thames within the ancient boundaries. In the picture above, flames from a bombed building in the City illuminate the night sky behind the dome of St. Paul's Cathedral, right. Actually, the Croydon Airport was the military objective, though the Nazis had given orders to bomb the City "if necessary."

247

The first bombs are dropped on the heart of London

FIREMEN TACKLE CITY BLAZE. On August 25, just after midnight, the first bombs were dropped on the City, causing a fire which gutted a large commercial building. Left, firemen are playing on the blaze from a water tower. Above, the fire under control. Several hundred bombs we dropped on and near London during five raids in the space of thirty hours, but the damage was small and of no importance.

The Nazis launch their first all-night raid on London

ALL-NIGHT RAID ON BRITAIN'S CAPITAL. Goering's air force launched its first all-night raid on London, when on the night of August 26 small waves of Nazi bombers operated repeatedly over the London area from 9.30 p.m. to 3.45 a.m. Though bombs were dropped in residential districts over a wide area, the resulting damage was small and out of all proportion to the "nuisance value" of the attack, and the main purpose of the raid seemed to be to hold up production by depriving workers of their sleep. The most illustrious victim claimed by the Nazis on this occasion was John Milton, whose statue outside the church where he is buried was blown from its pedestal by bomb blast and slightly damaged. A.R.P. workers are seen (left, below) tending the poet's wounds. Left (above), the wreckage of a Heinkel bomber which fell in flames in the garden of a bungalow on London's outskirts without, however, injuring the occupants. Searchlights sweeping the heavens in chase of the marauders (above) gave Londoners a vivid display of sky patterns.

Dive bombing attack on the white cliffs of Folkestone

RESORT TOWN BOMBED. On August 26, three waves of enemy bombers and fighters carried out raids on South-east England, especially over Portsmouth, the Thames Estuary and Folkestone. In the latter town a formation of about twenty planes dive bombed to about 500 feet, machine gunning streets, demolishing several houses on the sea front, and securing two direct hits on a laundry where three persons were killed.

The raiders were immediately attacked by British fighter pilots, assisted by Canadian squadrons and also by the newly formed Czech air force. Four enemy planes were shot down and altogether the day's bag amounted to at least forty-six enemy craft brought down against a loss of fifteen British fighters, eleven of whose pilots were saved by their parachutes. The picture shows bombs bursting over Folkestone.

Indian and South African troops rally to the colors

JOIN THE FIGHT FOR FREEDOM. As the first year of the war drew to a close more and more of the British Empire's man-power was mobilized to swell the ranks of those who were engaged in the struggle for freedom. Many troops from territories overseas were already in England awaiting the long-expected invader, whilst others in remote corners of the earth were mustering their strength to join battle when

the call came. Early in August the first detachments of the South African Field Force arrived in East Africa. Below (left) South African soldiers parading to hear an address by General Smuts, the Union Premier, on the eve of embarkation for the north; (right), a loaded transport about to depart from a Union port. Above, Indian troops from the State of Patiala being reviewed before leaving India for active service overseas.

EUROPE
AFTER ONE YEAR OF WAR

AXIS POWERS   SEPT. I 1939
AXIS POWERS   OCCUPIED TERRITORY   SEPT. I 1940
RUSSIAN OCCUPIED TERRITORY SEPT. I 1940
BULGARIAN OCCUPIED TERRITORY   SEPT. I 1940
BOUNDARIES SEPT. I 1939 ———— BOUNDARIES SEPT. I 1940 ------

SCALE OF MILES   0   100   200   300   400   500   600   700

WAR CHANGES THE FACE OF TWO CONTINENTS. When war broke out in September, 1939, Germany already had been responsible for several changes in the map of Europe. Austria, Czechoslovakia and Memel had been incorporated within the Third Reich. After the outbreak of war Poland was overrun and shared between Germany and Russia, and the latter widened her frontier still further after the war with Finland. Then, in April, Germany occupied Norway and Denmark and in the following two months overran most of France and the Low Countries in a lightning campaign. In June, Russia demanded Bessarabia and

NORTH AFRICA

ITALIAN EMPIRE	
BRITISH EMPIRE	
FRENCH EMPIRE	

MILES   0   500   1000

S·J·Turner, F.R.G.S.

Bukovina from Rumania and occupied these areas on the 28th. Russia won a political rather than geographical victory in July, when the Baltic States Estonia, Latvia and Lithuania, over which she had been steadily increasing her influence, decided to become Soviet republics. In August, Rumania was forced to cede more territory; she handed over Southern Dobruja to Bulgaria and agreed to cede about sixty per cent of Transylvania to Hungary. Hungary, however, had not occupied this area by the end of the first year of the war. In Africa, the Italians were in control of French Somaliland and had occupied British Somaliland.

THE SECOND YEAR

AFTER France fell, the British Isles became the next Nazi objective. Every schoolboy knew that Hitler's next blow would be struck at the English homeland. Hitler, himself, confirmed this by boasting that he would be in London by mid-August, 1940. Britain faced one of the great crises of her history, and the Battle of Britain that followed deserves to be ranked with the crucial actions of Waterloo and Marathon.

The outline of the German plan became apparent a month after the French surrender. Hitler intended first to "soften up" British resistance by air raids on the ports and vital centers, and then to try an invasion. The air attack actually started in July, 1940. It continued with steady intensity until January, 1941, when bad weather curtailed operations. The fierce tempo was resumed in March and continued through April, May, and early June, after which Hitler gave up the Battle of Britain to operate in other fields.

England was not invaded because Germany failed to establish mastery of the air over the island. After Dunkirk, the British aircraft industry got down to a mass production basis. Men of the R.A.F. proved themselves technically superior to their adversaries, and usually were victorious in any battle of equal odds. By January, 1941, 3,437 German planes had been shot down as compared to 847 British machines. Another important fact is that a large percentage of the British flyers parachuted to safety, whereas the loss of a German plane meant the loss of the entire crew.

The first phase of the Battle of Britain was marked by German concentration on military prey. It ended on August 15, 1940 by a decisive German defeat when 180 of 1,000 Nazi planes were lost in a single day. The strict attention to military objectives was then abandoned for indiscriminate bombing, calculated to break the hearts of the English. London was first badly hit September 7, and from then until the following June it served as a constant target for Nazi planes.

While the loss of life during this period never reached critical proportions, property damage was enormous. Statistics issued by the Ministry of Home Security show that from August, 1940 to January, 1941, 22,744 civilians were killed and 31,817 injured in raids over England. In March, April, and May of 1941, when the Reich again resumed the fury of its attacks, the number killed was 15,949 and the injured 16,901. Property damage for all England was placed at $480,000,000 for the first two years of the war.

ITALIAN DISASTER

THE early months of the second year of the war tell the story of Italian military and naval incompetency. The drive towards the Suez Canal from Libya which had begun with great fanfare in August of 1940 abruptly petered out in September. Sidi Barrani was taken, but there the Italian attack stalled, only 70 miles east of the Libyan border.

On October 28, Mussolini launched an invasion of Greece from Albanian soil which he had "conquered" early in 1939, before the beginning of World War II. The Greeks looked to be helpless as the Italians began pouring over the Albanian border. The Greek first line troops numbered no more than 150,000, poorly equipped according to the requirements of modern warfare. The Greek Navy consisted of one obsolete cruiser, ten destroyers, thirteen torpedo boats and six submarines.

The world now knows how well the Greeks defended their homeland. Within a month of the start of the invasion, not an Italian soldier remained on Greek soil. The Greeks had launched a counter-offensive and were soon waging war in Albania, taking the important Italian bases of Koritza, Argirocastro, and, ironically enough, Porto Edda which had been renamed for Mussolini's daughter. By the end of 1940 they were in possession of one-fourth of Albanian soil, and had driven the Italians from all important ports except Valona and Durazzo.

On the night of November 11-12, a British task force accomplished the initial deflation of Mussolini's claim to control of the Mediterranean Sea. The main part of the Italian battle fleet was caught fast asleep in the harbor of Taranto, and when the one-sided action was over, three of Il Duce's six capital ships were out of service. British raids on Italian convoys bound for Libya were correspondingly successful, and the conclusion became inescapable that Mussolini had lost control of the Mediterranean, presuming he had ever held it.

In December, the British army pushed the Italians out of Egypt, recapturing Sidi Barrani and marching into Libya to take Bardia, Tobruk and Bengazi in the early months of 1941. England had won the first phase of the battle of Cyrenaica, a barren, sandy wasteland that was to become the scene of fluctuating fortunes for both the democracies and the Axis.

The assault on the Italian East African Empire was made from both the Anglo-Egyptian Sudan and Kenya. Cooperating with the British, Haile Selassie, the Ethiopian monarch, had returned to his former domain and mobilized large bodies of loyal natives. The first victories came in March when the Kenya divisions not only took Italian Somaliland but recaptured British Somaliland. On April 6 British troops took the Ethiopian capital of Addis Ababa and restored Haile Selassie to his throne. In May the dissolution of the Italian East African Empire was completed by the conquest of Eritrea.

THE BALKAN CAMPAIGN

GERMANY'S next full-fashioned offensive was directed against the Balkan states. With Rumania, Bulgaria and Hungary safely enrolled under the Axis banner, only Yugoslavia and Greece remained to be taken. Hitler's other purpose was to rescue Mussolini from a bad predicament in Albania.

The new blitzkrieg began on April 6 with simultaneous marches against Yugoslavia and Greece, the latter of which had been bolstered by a British expeditionary force. By April 17 Yugoslavia was beaten, although small native units continued an effective guerrilla warfare. The Greeks with their English allies held out until April 28. By May 1 the British had evacuated to the island of Crete which they had occupied with Greece's consent in October 1940. On May 19, Germany's troops landed on Crete, and by June 1 had dislodged the British in what was one of the bloodiest phases of the war. Mussolini was saved from his Albanian plight, and once more the British were without a foothold on the European continent.

THE MIDDLE EAST

IN late April the British took the first step to clean up Axis agent activity in the middle east. This region, rich in oil deposits, had presented a tempting plum to the greedy Wehrmacht. In Iraq, Raaschid Ali Beg Gailani had overthrown the regency, ruling for the four-year old monarch, Feisal II. Gailani surrounded himself with Italian and German henchmen who cooperated with agents in Syria where the Vichy-controlled government showed no disposition to curb their ingenuity. On May 2, Iraq artillery opened fire on a British garrison at the Habania airport, precipitating a campaign which ended on May 30 when the British occupied Bagdad. British and French troops marched against the Vichy French in Syria on June 8. The capital of Damascus fell to the invaders on June 21, although the Vichy French commander, Henry Dentz, delayed final surrender until July 14. Vichy France gave up the Syrian and Lebanon mandate and turned over this territory to the protection of the British and Free French.

GERMANY STRIKES AT RUSSIA

RUMBLINGS of discord between Germany and Russia struck a critical note early in June of 1941. After she had subdued Finland, Russia, in 1940, had acquired the Baltic states of Estonia, Latvia and Lithuania, and Rumania's Bessarabia. The first three were the awards of plebiscites, and the gift of Bessarabia was the result of diplomatic pressure. In the first weeks of June heavy troop concentrations were established on both sides of the frontier by both the Axis and the Russians. For some weeks Nazi units had been garrisoned in Finland, and Germany had offered no plausible explanation for their presence.

Then, on June 22, Germany suddenly struck at Russia, somewhat altering her usual routine by a formal declaration of war which spoke of the "Bolshevik menace to civilized Europe." While the German attack was generally directed at all points on the huge front, three main spearheads developed after the first days of fighting. One struck from German-occupied Poland and East Prussia into Lithuania, with the Baltic States and Leningrad as the ultimate objective. A second worked out of German Poland into Russian Poland in the direction of Moscow. A third, composed of Nazi and Rumanian troops, invaded Bessarabia with the rich Ukraine as its goal.

During the first three weeks, Lithuania, Latvia, Russian Poland were taken and White Russia invaded. In the south Bessarabia was once returned to Rumanian rule. From Minsk northwards, the advance averaged 300 miles— a formidable accomplishment when viewed from any standpoint. But by now the mobilization of Russia had been completed, and while the Reich continued to press forward, the progress was slower and more costly.

In the north the Germans reached the outskirts of Leningrad by late August. In their attack on this historic city, they were aided by the Finns who had again taken up arms and, with Nazi divisions, were surging down the Karelian Isthmus. In the central sector Russia admitted the fall of Smolensk on August 13, and the Germans were pressing towards Moscow. In the south they reached Odessa in mid-August, encountered a stiff resistance, and then by-passed the city in an advance on Kiev, the capital and largest city of the Ukraine.

To keep open the supply lines into Russia, British and Russian forces engineered a joint invasion of Iran in August. They forced the abdication of pro-Axis Shah Riza in favor of his son Prince Mohammed, a potentate of democratic sympathies.

AFTER THE RAIDERS HAD GONE. Although Germany's daylight raiders met with little success in their attacks on London, those that came by night succeeded in causing considerable damage to property, besides killing and injuring many civilians. This view of the approach to London Bridge is a typical example of the scenes of devastation that greeted city workers on the way to their offices the morning after a raid.

Second phase of the battle of Britain

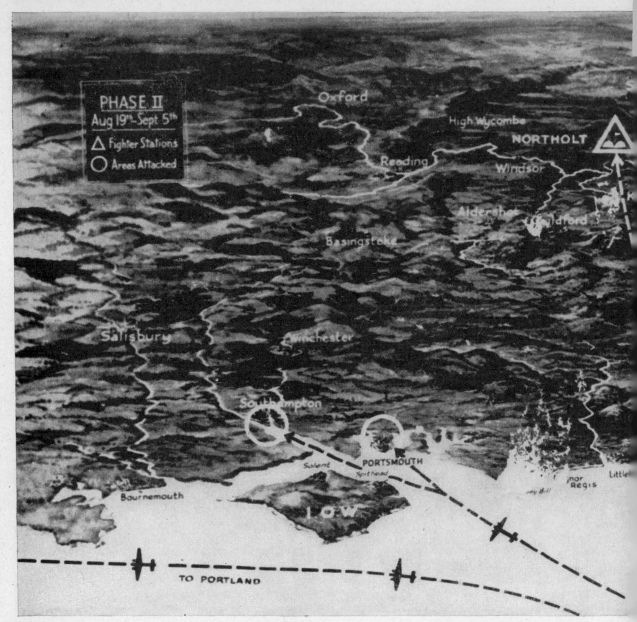

LUFTWAFFE'S ATTACKS ON FIGHTER BASES. A short lull of five days, filled by reconnaissance flights in which thirty-nine German planes were shot down, separated the second phase of the Battle of Britain from the first. From August 24 to September 5 the main weight of the German attack was directed against fighter stations and airplane factories inland. During the first six days of this action heavy attacks were directed on Portland, Southampton, Portsmouth, Dover and Folkestone, areas in Kent and Essex, and the Thames Estuary; on August 30 and the succeeding days the airfields on the London outskirts and in Kent were the chief objectives. Although damage was done to the airfields attacked, the attempt to put the British fighter squadrons out of action was a complete failure; and, whether from a determination to stick to a prearranged time-

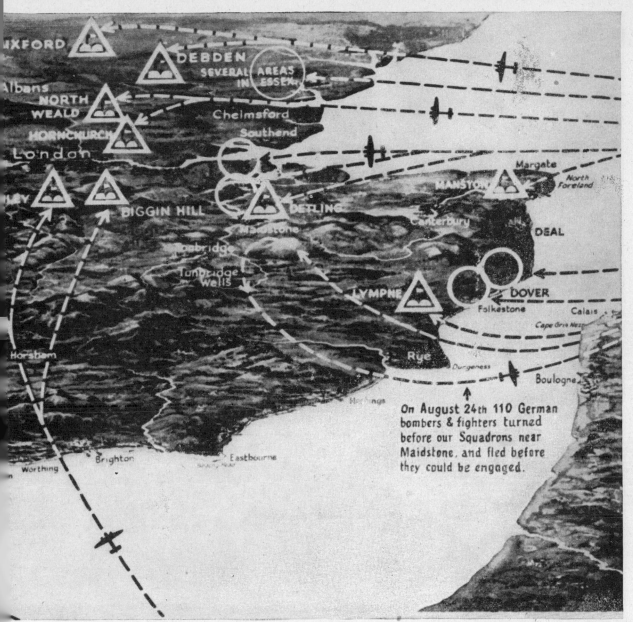

On August 24th 110 German bombers & fighters turned before our Squadrons near Maidstone, and fled before they could be engaged.

table, or because it was wrongly supposed that sufficient damage had been done to make the R.A.F. incapable of defending London, this phase of the struggle was closed on September 5. Thirty-five main attacks were made during this stage of the battle; they resulted in a loss of 562 German bombers and fighters: probably hundreds more shared their fate, for the official score included only cases of certain destruction. British losses were 219 aircraft; but the pilots of these were saved in 132 cases. The objectives of this stage are shown in the map above, reproduced from the British Ministry of Information booklet, "The Battle of Britain." It was carried through with smaller bomber formations than those previously employed, with larger fighter escorts, the latter flying partly at great height, round and slightly above the bombers.

TURMOIL IN RUMANIA. Unrest in Rumania had grown rapidly since her government, in June, ceded Bessarabia and Northern Bukovina, with a combined population of about four millions, to the U.S.S.R. In August, Nazi pressure had forced her to give up Southern Dobruja to Bulgaria, and, a week later, to restore to Hungary about two-thirds of Transylvania, annexed after the last war. Widespread rioting, in which the Fascist Iron Guard played a prominent part, took place all over the country, and on the morning of September 6 King Carol abdicated in favour of his eighteen-year-old son Michael. The Premier, General Antonescu, who assumed dictatorial powers as Conductor or Leader, is seen (above) addressing a meeting, with a small group of green-shirted Iron Guards standing at attention below. Next to him stands the Iron Guard leader, Horea Sima. The portrait above the dais is that of Codreanu, the former Iron Guard leader, shot "while attempting to escape" when under arrest for causing an uprising against the former regime. Below, Iron Guard legionaires, side by side with men in native dress, are marching through a square in Bucharest.

The Union Jack goes up on 50 U. S. destroyers September 7, 1940

NAVAL AID FROM AMERICA FOR BRITAIN. The first batch of the fifty destroyers handed over to Great Britain by agreement with the U.S.A. arrived at a Canadian port on September 7. Above, American and Canadian sailors fraternize on the deck of one of the ships; below, Canadian officers and men on their way to take over one of the destroyers.

DOCKLAND RAID THROUGH GERMAN EYES. Long before the war, the Germans had claimed that, if they wished, they could in a few hours reduce the whole of East London's docks and riverside areas to a heap of blazing rubble. On September 7, with a force of about 400 bombers, they did their best to carry out their threat. Their own official photographs, one of which is seen above, show that the effects of the raids, serious as they were, fell very far short of their hopes. Thanks to the R.A.F., the attempt to treat London as Rotterdam had been served did not succeed—and its cost was 114 German planes destroyed in two days.

AMERICA'S MOUNTING AID. As the months passed, American public opinion became increasingly convinced that the freedom of the United States and the future of democracy depended upon the victory of the Allied cause. The wheels of American industry moved faster and faster, and, as war production got into its stride, the quantity of supplies for the British forces continually rose. A train of whippet tanks, purchased by the Canadian Government for use at Canadian Tank Corps training grounds, is here seen arriving at Camp Borden, Canada. Some of them bore chalked messages from America, such as "Good luck, Canada."

Empire troops reinforce Britain's armies in the Middle East

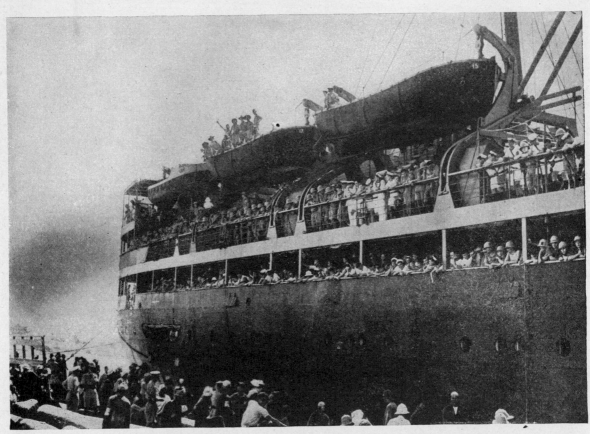

PREPARING FOR ATTACK ON ITALY'S EMPIRE. During the first part of the operations in the Western Desert, a small British mobile force had completely dominated the eastern frontier of Libya in face of greatly superior Italian forces, and full plans had been made to meet the enemy attack when it should come. Units of French Colonial infantry under General Charles de Gaulle's banner were formed to share in the defense

of Egypt. Meanwhile Britain's growing forces were heavily reinforced during September, numerous detachments of land troops and airmen from Great Britain, India, Australia and New Zealand being disembarked at ports in the Middle East. The upper picture shows Indian troops after disembarking from a transport; below, left, a troopship coming alongside to discharge troops; right, airmen disembarking with their kit.

HOW BRITAIN HIT BACK. The R.A.F. paid frequent visits to Berlin, often staying for several hours over the city, which contained many military objectives. On September 10 the Germans admitted that hits were scored on the Reichstag and the garden of Joseph Paul Goebbels' home. Above, German Safety Service workers putting out a fire started by British incendiary bombs; below, civilians clearing away the debris after a night raid on Germany's capital.

RAIDER'S FEAT AND RAIDER'S FATE. In the early morning of September 10, a delayed action bomb caused extensive damage at King George's London home. Five days later another bomb hit the palace. Above, the King and Queen are seen inspecting the damage. The shop outside Victoria Station (below) was demolished by a raider—believed to be the plane that bombed Buckingham Palace on the 15th—which fell on the roof of the shop in flames.

SEPTEMBER 13, 1940: ITALIANS INVADE EGYPT. Mussolini's troops began their long-awaited advance into Egypt early in September, and on the 13th they crossed the frontier and occupied El Sollum. Here Italian troops are seen advancing across the desert under a covering barrage from their artillery.

Italy faces Britain on the soil of Egypt

CAMPAIGN IN THE DESERT. After occupying Sollum and the customs post of El Musaid on September 13, the Italian forces, consisting of infantry, mechanized units, Blackshirt units and camel corps, penetrated a few miles further into the trackless and waterless desert by way of Wadi Halfaya, nicknamed by the British "Hellfire Pass." Artillery fire caused them heavy losses. The British deliberately withdrew before the Italian advance in order to tempt the enemy into a dangerous lengthening of their lines of communication. Meanwhile the Duce's troops were constantly harried by tanks and the R.A.F., and by the Fleet's guns from the sea. The pictures show: above, Italian soldiers supported by caterpillar-pulled artillery advancing near El Sollum; below, left, British tank crews "cleaning up" in the Western desert; center, Italian machine gunners taking cover in shallow trenches near El Sollum; right, an Italian desert "spotter" looking out for the dreaded raiding parties of British tanks.

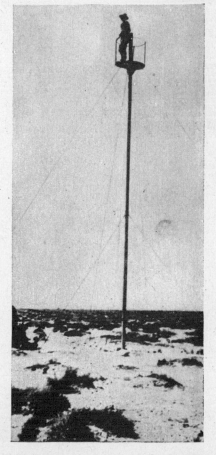

275

ATTACKS ON GERMAN COASTAL GUNS. The big German guns that bombarded Dover and British convoys in the Channel were regularly subjected to intense bombardment both by the R.A.F. and long-range guns on the British coast. The enemy emplacements were cunningly camouflaged and strongly guarded by anti-aircraft guns which put up a fierce barrage whenever British planes appeared (above). Below, bomb and shell damage in a French coastal town that was unfortunate enough to harbor a "Big Bertha."

THWARTING THE INVASION MENACE. Hitler's repeated threats to invade Britain remained threats as yet—thanks in large measure, no doubt, to the good work put in by British bombers. While their brothers of the Fighter Command battled against enemy raiders in the skies above Britain, they flew across to the French, Dutch and Belgian ports almost nightly to upset the results of the Germans' day's work. Special attention was paid to the troop-carrying barges which lay ready for a swoop on the English coast. This British official photograph shows the dock area at Dunkirk, where many of the invasion barges were concentrated, after a visit from the Royal Air Force. Damaged barges can be seen near the entrance to the upper dock; the warehouses surrounding it are completely destroyed, while two big buildings facing the other dock have been demolished and the center one gutted. The wharves and sidings are pitted with bomb craters.

British fighter pilots shoot down 185 Nazi raiders over Britain

BRITAIN'S AERIAL TRAFALGAR. September 15 marked the climax of the Battle of Britain. On that day 500 German aircraft, 250 in the morning and 250 in the afternoon, made a most determined attempt to reach London. "Spitfires" and "Hurricanes" that went up to intercept the enemy broke up the raiding formations and the battle developed into a series of running fights. By the end of the day the British pilots had accounted for 185 enemy planes, and unofficial estimates raised the Nazi loss to 232. British losses were twenty-five planes, thirteen of whose pilots were saved. The picture shows a Hurricane giving a victorious sweep over the relics of its victim, a Heinkel 111 bomber, shot down in one of the encounters of the day.

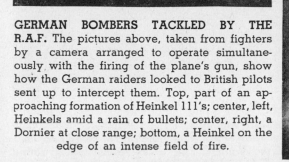

GERMAN BOMBERS TACKLED BY THE R.A.F. The pictures above, taken from fighters by a camera arranged to operate simultaneously with the firing of the plane's gun, show how the German raiders looked to British pilots sent up to intercept them. Top, part of an approaching formation of Heinkel 111's; center, left, Heinkels amid a rain of bullets; center, right, a Dornier at close range; bottom, a Heinkel on the edge of an intense field of fire.

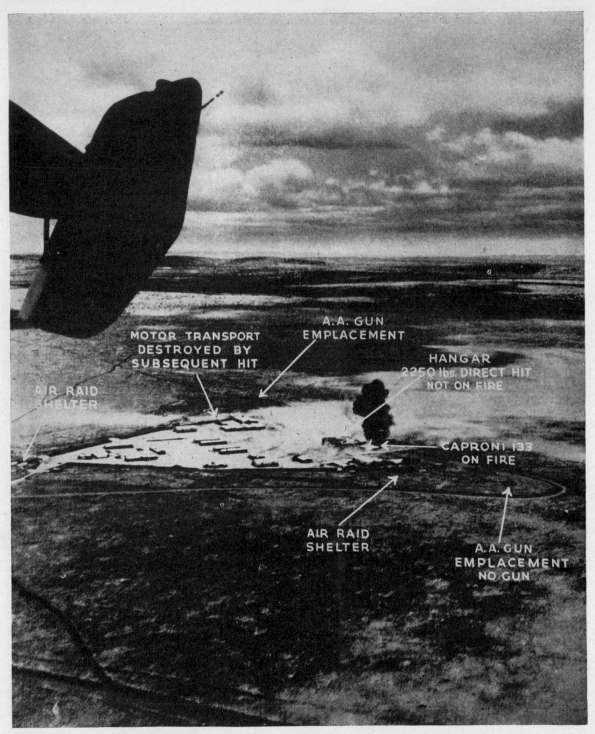

AIR RAID
SHELTER

MOTOR TRANSPORT
DESTROYED BY
SUBSEQUENT HIT

A.A. GUN
EMPLACEMENT

HANGAR
2250 lbs. DIRECT HIT
NOT ON FIRE

CAPRONI 133
ON FIRE

AIR RAID
SHELTER

A.A. GUN
EMPLACEMENT
NO GUN

ATTACKING ITALY'S AFRICAN EMPIRE. Large-scale air attacks on Italy's possessions in Somaliland, Eritrea and Abyssinia by South African and British airmen were continuous during September. Much damage was done to the Jibuti-Addis Ababa railway, and countless hits were scored on air fields and other military objectives. In the picture a dense column of smoke is seen rising from a Caproni bomber set on fire by a bomb at one of these airfields. A hangar beside the column of smoke was destroyed by two direct hits.

The de Gaulle expedition to Dakar September 23-25, 1940

FREE FRENCH OFF WEST AFRICA. General de Gaulle, leader of the Free French, arrived off Dakar on September 23 with a small naval and military force. He hoped to enlist the support of the Colony against the Vichy government's policy of co-operation with Germany and persuade it to rally to the Free French standard. British ships stood by, but de Gaulle's attempt at a peaceful landing was resisted, and after two days he decided to withdraw rather than cause a fight between Frenchmen. British ships came into action, and two submarines which attacked them were sunk. The pictures show: above, General de Gaulle conferring with his officers before the withdrawal; below, French officers putting off to meet the French Governor-general. The launch was fired on during its journey.

R.A.F. HAVOC AT GERMAN NAVAL BASE. The harbor of Kiel, at the eastern end of the Kaiser Wilhelm Canal, Germany's most important naval port and dockyard, afforded an excellent target for the R.A.F., and one which they very frequently visited. Several large-scale attacks were made on it during September, resulting in considerable damage to shipping docked or under construction, and the results of the raids were evidenced by air photographs taken at various stages of the attacks. That reproduced above was taken two days after a particularly heavy raid in which much damage was done, and bombs were observed to fall close to the Scharnhorst, Germany's crack 26,000-ton battleship, seen in floating dock at (1) in the picture. Other reference numbers indicate: (2) A 19,250-ton aircraft-carrier, not yet completed. (3) The heavy

OUTER DOCKYARD BASIN

NAVAL ARSENAL

cruiser Lutzow, in dry dock, undergoing repairs to her stern. (4) A 10,000-ton crusier of the Hipper class, also being repaired. (5) A smaller cruiser, in the repairers' hands. (6) Three submarines. (7) Two cruiser mine-layers. (8) Four torpedo-boats. (9) Three more submarines. (10) Two sail training ships. (11) A destroyer, in dry dock, undergoing repair. (12, 13, 15, 17) Tankers. (14, 16) Liners. (18) Destroyer, under construction. (19) Submarine, in floating dock. (20) Two submarines. (21) Light cruiser, under construction. (22) Submarine, in floating dock. (23) The target ship Zahringen. (24) "E"-boats. Damage was also done to oil, torpedo and gun stores, and to the Central Power Station of the Deutsche Werke yard. Photographs taken a few days later showed that the Scharnhorst was undergoing repairs as a result of injuries sustained in the raids.

A Sunderland sinks an Italian submarine September, 1940

WATCHDOGS OF THE R.A.F. The planes and flying boats of the Coastal Command constantly patrolled vast areas of sea on the lookout for enemy U-boats and surface raiders lying in wait for British convoys. Altogether during 1940 they flew some twenty-five million miles and escorted more than 2,000 convoys, including approximately 40,000 ships carrying cargoes valued at an average of £4,000,000 per day. The Sunderland flying boat seen above has just bombed and sunk an Italian submarine while on patrol in the Mediterranean. All that can be seen of the under-water raider is a large patch of bubbles in the sea below.

TRIPARTITE TREATY SIGNED IN BERLIN. On September 27, 1940, Japan, whose sympathies lay with Germany and Italy, signed a ten-year pact with these two countries. This provided for mutual aid in the event of any of the signatories being attacked by a power not so far involved in the war, and was interpreted as a warning to the United States. The picture above shows: left to right, seated, Ciano (Italy), Ribbentrop (Germany) and Saburo Kuruso (Japanese Ambassador to Germany) signing agreement. On the left, Japanese officers on a mission to Germany inspecting captured Maginot Line.

World famous London thoroughfares damaged in September raids

HOLBORN

ADE!

STRAND

OX

LACE

REGENT STREET

THE NATIONAL BANK

EET

TEMPLE

BOMB BLAST AT WESTMINSTER. Throughout the autumn, the nightly rain of high explosive bombs on London continued and many famous buildings suffered damage. Among them were the Houses of Parliament, one window of which, as seen above, has been damaged by the blast of a nearby bomb and has lost much of its tracery. Marochetti's statue of Richard Lionheart defies the enemy with sword bent.

PARISH CHURCH OF THE EMPIRE STRUCK. Historic St. Paul's Cathedral, saved from destruction in September by the heroic work of Lieut. Davies and his bomb disposal squad, continued to be a military objective for Nazi planes. In October it was seriously damaged by a high explosive bomb which pierced the roof and fell close to the High Altar, which as this picture shows, was reduced to a heap of rubble.

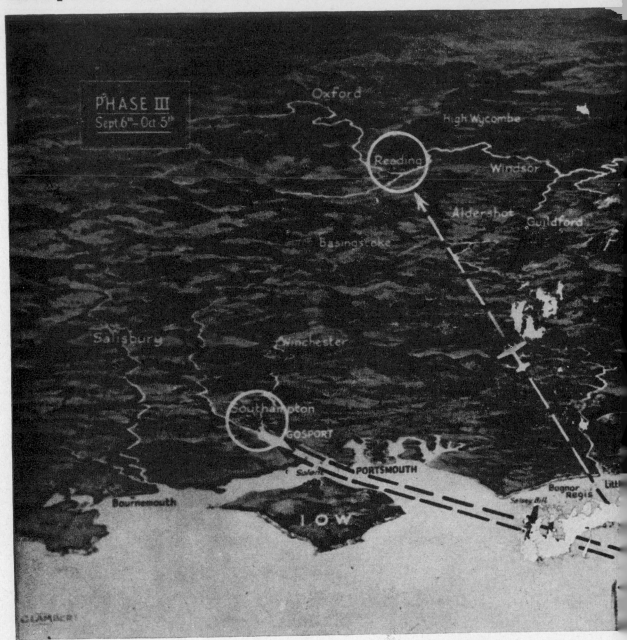

PHASE III
Sept 6th – Oct 5th

LONDON BECOMES LUFTWAFFE'S MAIN TARGET. The third stage of the Battle of Britain opened on September 6, its first spectacular exploit being the mass attack on the London dockland area. From the beginning of this phase to its end on October 5, thirty-eight major daytime attacks were delivered, apart from the almost incessant night raids on the capital. Much damage was inflicted on private property, communications, and public utility services, but objectives of military importance suffered very little harm. The high-water mark of this phase of the contest came in the two great attacks on September 15 when the Germans lost 185 aircraft (see page 278). During the mass attacks dive bombers sought to create diversions by bombing shipping and coastal objectives in Essex and Kent. The fighter escorts of the attackers were in-

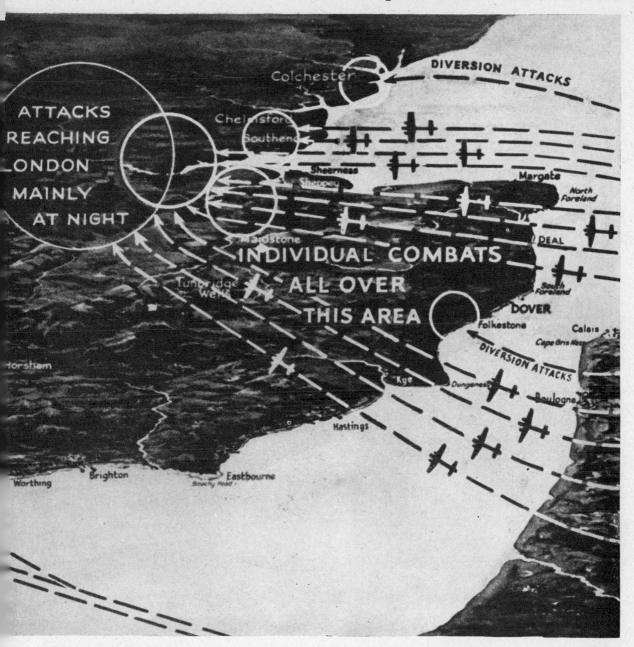

creased in number, and endeavored to draw off the defending R.A.F. fighter planes by flying high above their companion bombers. The R.A.F.'s reply to these tactics was for Spitfire squadrons to engage the high-flying fighter screen between London and the coast, while Hurricanes attacked the bombers before they reached the airfields in the London district. As the attacks continued, the proportion of German to British losses rose higher and higher; on September 27 one R.A.F. group destroyed 99 German aircraft for the loss of sixteen British pilots, while on October 5 only one pilot was shot down for an enemy loss of sixteen planes. The total loss of enemy planes in this third phase of the combat amounted to 883 aircraft. The map above, reproduced from "The Battle of Britain," shows the direction and objectives of the main and diversion attacks.

FRENCH COLONIES ADHERE TO DE GAULLE. Undaunted by lack of success at Dakar, the Free French leader continued to receive the adhesion of other French colonies in Africa and elsewhere to the cause of liberty. On October 10 his standard was raised at Duala, the capital of French Cameroon. The upper picture was taken as his expedition came alongside the quay at that town; below, troops pledged to the Free French cause parade for a memorial ceremony at Noumea, New Caledonia, French island in the South Pacific.

ENEMY SHIPS BATTERED IN NORMAN PORT. One of the most successful of the many remarkable operations against the Channel ports was the Royal Navy's attack on a concentration of enemy shipping at Cherbourg, carried out in close co-operation with the R.A.F. An intense night bombardment by heavy and light naval units resulted in a large number of fires in the dock area. Havoc was wrought among the enemy vessels anchored in the harbor as the salvos from the British ships burst on their targets.

An Italian destroyer loses battle with a British ship

BRITISH NAVAL SUCCESS IN MEDITERRANEAN. On October 12, H.M.S. Ajax, which played a leading part in the battle of the River Plate, intercepted and sank two Italian destroyers off Sicily. A little later, she met a force comprising a heavy cruiser and four destroyers, one of them, the 1,620-ton Artigliere, of the latest class. The Ajax after crippling this vessel was joined by H.M.S. York, but lost her prey during the

night. Next morning Artigliere was located in tow of another Italian destroyer, which deserted her charge. The Artigliere's crew was ordered to abandon ship, after which she was sunk by the York. The pictures show: top, left, the doomed ship after her crew have taken off; bottom, left, York's first salvo hits Artigliere; top, right, another shell striking the Italian vessel; bottom, right, the explosion after a direct hit.

MORE MOVES ON DIPLOMATIC FRONT. On October 23, in search of new Axis partners, Hitler met the Spanish dictator General Francisco Franco (top, left) on the Spanish border, and the next day met Marshal Petain whom he is greeting (bottom) in France. The Vichy government afterwards announced that the German and French leaders had "agreed in principle" on collaboration. The meeting with the Spanish leader produced little result. Top, right, Hitler and Mussolini at the Palazzo Vecchio, Florence.

CARRYING ON. Loss of sleep, nights in underground shelters, homelessness—nothing could take the smile from Londoners' faces. After a raid they came out from their refuge to salvage whatever could be salvaged of their treasured possessions—even if it were only a clock or an aspidistra plant.

The Empress of Britain sinks after attack by dive bombers

C. P. R. FLAGSHIP DESTROYED. The Empress of Britain, crack 42,000-ton liner of the Canadian Pacific fleet was attacked by enemy aircraft on October 26, about 150 miles off the Irish coast. After machine gunning the liner's crew the German dive bombers registered direct hits with both high explosives and incendiary bombs, leaving the vessel a blazing wreck (right). The tugs on the left attempted to tow her

to port, but the effort was unsuccessful, and the liner, with flames belching from her funnels, blew up and sank in the darkness. Some 600 of the 643 persons aboard, for the most part soldiers' wives and families, were picked up and brought to port by rescue vessels. Among the men saved from the sea was her commander, Captain Sapsworth, C.V.O., who remained with his ship until she went down.

Italy invades Greece from Albania

GREEKS REJECT ITALIAN ULTIMATUM. Italy, alleging violations of Greek neutrality, presented a three-hour ultimatum to Greece on October 28, demanding that certain unspecified strategical points be conceded. The Greek Premier, Gen. Metaxas, received this as a declaration of war. An Italian attack was immediately launched. The pictures show: top, left, Greek troops on guard at the frontier a few days before war was declared; right, Greek troops in action near the frontier; bottom, left, Italian cavalry riding into Greece; right, Greek warships which shelled the Italian forces near the coast as they sought to cross the Albanian border.

London landmarks hit by bombs of the German raiders

(1)

(3)

(2)

THE BATTLE OF LONDON.

Throughout October the Nazi attack on London continued in a fruitless endeavor to break the spirit of its people, and to raze their homes and historic buildings to the ground. The "military objectives" attacked by the Germans included hospitals, churches, museums, the offices of commercial organizations, theaters and restaurants, mansions, apartments, and the working-class dwellings of the little streets. Typical scenes of those memorable days are depicted in these photographs. They show (1) "The Times" office, in Queen Victoria Street, its windows and much of its walls damaged by blast, but with its flags

still bravely flying. (2) The Dutch Church, Austin-Friars, dating from before London's first Great Fire in 1666, completely ruined and burnt out. (3) The library of Holland House, Lord Ilchester's Kensington mansion, once the home of Charles James Fox, which with the exception of one wing was completely destroyed. (4) St. Clement Danes, the famous church in the Strand, badly damaged by blast from a heavy bomb. (5) Damage in Middle Temple Hall opened by Queen Elizabeth in 1562. (6) Leicester Square, (7) The main hall of Stationers' Hall, showing the Caxton window, (8) Pensioners surveying bomb damage at the Chelsea Hospital.

GENERAL SMUTS IN THE FIELD. In October and November General Smuts made a tour of inspection of South African troops at their advanced training camps in East Africa, where they were preparing for forthcoming operations against the Italians in Abyssinia, Eritrea and British Somaliland. The pictures show: above, troops giving their premier a rousing reception after hearing a speech from him during his visit; below, part of a troop-carrying convoy of highly mechanized South African units in Kenya.

Greeks slow down the Italian invader November 1-2, 1940

ITALIAN ADVANCE IN GREECE HELD. Italian troops that invaded Greek territory had been promised an easy victory by the Duce, but within the first few days they were to learn that they were opposed by a brave and resolute enemy who could take full advantage of the difficult and rugged country. The pictures, taken during the early days of the campaign, show: above, Italians retreating along a mountain road after a Greek counter-attack; below, Greek infantry on the march to take up their positions in the line.

British rally to the support of an old friend

BRITISH SUPPORT FOR INVADED GREECE. Before the war began Britain and France had promised to aid Greece if attacked. Britain's promise was at once kept and air and land forces were disembarked in Greece and Crete to support her in her struggle for freedom. The pictures show: top, left, British troops and tanks being blessed by a Cretan bishop as they pass through a town in the island; bottom, crowds in a Greek town watching a newly-arrived British mechanized column; top right, General Sir Archibald Wavell (in center) visiting a gun position in course of erection by British troops; bottom, R.A.F. personnel, with their kit, are shown arriving in Greece.

Nazi troops prepare for the invasion of Britain

HITLER THREATENS BUT DOESN'T COME. Continual threats of an imminent invasion of Britain appeared in the German Press and the speeches of German leaders, and German land forces trained intensively for the difficult job of getting and keeping a foothold on British shores. Left, Nazi soldiers are scaling cliffs over terrain such as they would meet on the English and Scottish coasts; a light gun team are seen hauling up their weapon. Right, above, Goering, with (left) Gen. Jeschonnek, Chief of the German Air Staff, and (right) Air Force Gen. Loerzer, making plans, with the aid of a map, for an attack on Britain. Below, a heavy bomb, which will fall on some British target, on its way to be loaded at an airfield in France.

Italian armies retreat before the Greeks in Albania

ITALIAN ADVANCE HALTED. The Italian thrust into Greece towards Salonika was held three miles over the frontier, and within a few days Greek troops, counterattacking, hurled the enemy back into Albania. By November 5 Koritza was within range of Greek mountain artillery. Meanwhile two Italian attacks further west, designed to encircle Yanina, were brought to a standstill by the Greeks. The pictures show: top, left, Italian troops in full retreat, their mechanical transport abandoned, urging on a mule wagon. Bottom, left, engineers building a temporary bridge to replace one destroyed by the R.A.F. Top, right, light tanks captured by the Greeks who used them against their former owners. Bottom, right, captured Italian mortars.

FORT GALLABAT RECAPTURED. Fort Gallabat, a post on the Abyssinia-Sudan frontier, was taken by the Italians in July. Early in November, however, British and Indian troops launched an attack on the post, which changed hands several times before falling to the British on November 7, the Italian forces retreating towards Metemma harassed by aerial bombardment. The pictures show: top, British troops in possession of the fort on the lookout for enemy movements; below, artillery shelling the fort before its final capture.

ITALIAN PLANES OVER BRITAIN. On Armistice Day Britain received the first large-scale visit from the Italian Air Force. Between fifteen and twenty bombers that appeared over the Thames Estuary, escorted by about sixty fighters, were routed by two Hurricane squadrons, who shot down eight bombers and five fighters without loss to themselves. Two of the planes, a Caproni bomber (above) and a Fiat C.R. 42 fighter (below), both of which crashed in Suffolk, are here shown. The remainder of the Italian formation fled.

The British strike a crippling blow at the Italian Navy

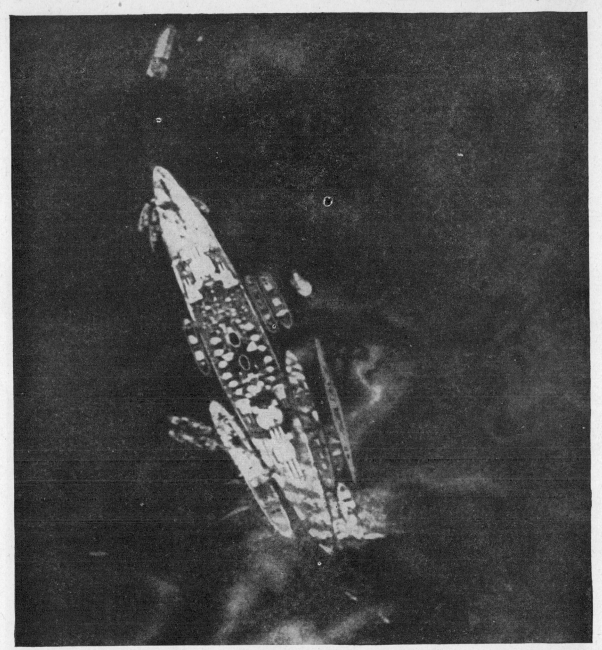

THE EXPLOIT AT TARANTO. On the night of November 11-12, a magnificently conceived attack on Italian capital ships in Taranto harbor was made by torpedo-carrying planes from the aircraft carriers Eagle and Illustrious. Its results decisively altered the balance of naval power in the Mediterranean. The British planes returned to their base leaving two battleships, one of the 35,000-ton Littorio class and one of the 23,000-ton Cavour class, partly under water and another Cavour class battleship severely damaged. Only two planes were lost in the action. The success of the attack was verified in subsequent reconnaissance flights by British planes, which showed that two of the damaged battleships were aground and the third apparently abandoned. Photographs taken during these flights show: on the left, above, a Cavour class battleship, her starboard side and her stern aft of the rear gun turrets submerged, beached on the outer harbor. Below, the inner harbor, with two damaged cruisers of the Trento class, and other warships; large quantities of fuel oil can be seen floating on the surface of the water. Above, a Littorio class battleship badly down by the bows, with salvage vessels and tugs and naval repair ships alongside.

Torpedo-carriers of the British fleet's air arm prove their worth

SOMETHING NEW IN MODERN WARFARE. Italy's fast but very shy navy always showed itself anxious to avoid meeting the British fleet in open battle. Admiral Sir Andrew Cunningham, commander of the British Mediterranean fleet, was therefore forced to destroy it while it lay at anchor at its base. In the "glorious episode of Taranto," to use Winston Churchill's words, he employed aircraft carriers, from the decks of which torpedo-carrying planes could take off to seek out the enemy. The success of the attack

proved beyond doubt the value of these ships, and brought fresh honor to the fleet air arm, whose offensive action against the Italians had already won them high praise. Torpedo-carriers can carry either a load of bombs or a single 18-in. torpedo. Left, one of these planes is seen releasing its "tin fish" during a practice flight. Right, above, a Swordfish, wings folded, passing down the aft well of its parent ship. Below, one of the planes circling round the aircraft-carrier Ark Royal preparatory to landing.

The Luftwaffe's ruthless attack on Coventry

WANTON DESTRUCTION OF COVENTRY. A ruthless attack was made by the Luftwaffe on Coventry on the night of November 14. Relays of bombers flew over the city from nightfall to dawn, dropping hundreds of tons of bombs indiscriminately and reducing the beautiful fourteenth-century Cathedral to a shapeless pile of stones. Churches, theatres, hospitals, public buildings, and many shops and houses in the business center and outskirts were destroyed or badly damaged. Left, the Cathedral spire, happily still standing, looks sadly down on the wreckage below; part of the walls and interior of the Cathedral are shown right (above), while below is seen the damaged font.

Coventry's shopping district a shambles after the Nazi raid

AFTER THE RAID. The German radio, gloating over the havoc wrought in Coventry by their bombers, coined a new word, "coventrated," to describe what their air force had done to the city. But the spirit

of the people of Coventry may be best judged from the mayor's remark on seeing the damage caused in the city (above): "We've always wanted a site for a new civic center," he said, "and now we have it."

KORITZA OCCUPIED. The Greek counter-attack in Eastern Albania pushed the Italians gradually but relentlessly back towards Koritza, and the capture of that town was announced by the Greek High Command on the 22nd. Many prisoners and numerous guns were captured. The pictures show: above, a Greek mule transport column moving along an Albanian mountain road; below, Greek troops preparing to bivouac for the night among the snow, whose rigors they could withstand far better than their foe.

BRITISH HELP ON ITS WAY. Britain's promised aid to Greece was not limited to support in the air. Many a convoy, such as that seen above, passed through Mussolini's "private" Mediterranean with stores and equipment for the Greek and British forces operating on the Albanian frontier. They were not immune from air attack, but Italian bombers seldom succeeded in inflicting on them anything more than "near misses." Below, the Ark Royal, Malaya and Renown, engaged on convoy duty, passing Gibraltar.

SEA BATTLE OFF SARDINIA. On November 27, British Naval and Fleet Air Arm forces made contact with two enemy battleships escorted by cruisers and destroyers to the west of Sardinia. Although the Italian ships opened fire, they soon broke off the action and retired, a cruiser, two destroyers and other vessels being seriously damaged before their escape. One British fighter plane was lost and the cruiser Berwick suffered slight damage. Above, a British destroyer firing at the Italian ships as enemy shells fall astern; below, a British destroyer and cruisers taking up positions before the engagement.

AIR TERROR IN THE BRITISH PROVINCES. After the conclusion of the Battle of Britain at the end of October, the German Air Force changed tactics and launched heavy night attacks on ports and industrial towns in the provinces. One of the most severe was a raid on Southampton on November 30. The business center of the city bore the brunt of the attack. Churches, shops, houses, a film theatre and a newspaper office were among the buildings hit. A few days later the King visited the stricken city. He is seen above, accompanied by Herbert Morrison, and the mayor of the city, inspecting the damage.

THE CHANGING FACE OF LONDON. By the end of November many of London's most famous landmarks, churches, hospitals, theatres, movies, stores, and other public buildings showed signs of the nightly air bombardment. A few of those damaged in November raids are shown here. Top left, part of the Tower of London after a raid—the eight-hundred-year-old walls appear to defy Hitler no less successfully than the steel and concrete of the twentieth century. Bottom, the famous and fashionable Church of St. James, Piccadilly. Top right, the Houses of Parliament, where damage was done to the cloisters and crypt; bottom, the auditorium of Drury Lane Theatre, where a bomb exploded in rear of the orchestra.

Anzacs in Egypt undergo intensive training in desert warfare

AUSTRALIANS PREPARE TO HIT BACK. Little news came from the Western Desert during November, though occasional minor engagements took place between advanced forces. Meanwhile the Anzacs carried out intensive maneuvers in readiness for the day when the order for serious attack on the Italian positions would be given. Above, Australians training with their Bren gun carriers in the desert; below, carriers moving up in battle formation for an assault; top right, infantry moving up in dispersed groups behind the carriers; bottom right, carriers negotiating a desert ridge.

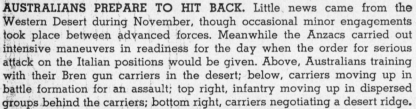

30 NOVEMBER—4 DECEMBER, 1940: ITALIANS BACK IN GREECE—AS PRISONERS. After the capture of Koritza, the Greeks pushed on in Eastern Albania towards Pogradets, the capture of which was announced on 30 November. Four days later came the news that the town of Premeti had fallen to the Greek Army advancing from the Pindus. Every day hundreds of prisoners fell, many of them willingly enough, into Greek hands. Here, in a Greek concentration camp, is a batch of them, lining up for rations.

SANTI QUARANTA OCCUPIED. Santi Quaranta, the Italians' southernmost Albania sea base was occupied on December 5, by the Greek Army advancing along the coastal road. On the same day the Italians evacuated Argyrokastro, which was entered by the Greeks, advancing through Delvino on the 8th. Many prisoners and great quantities of war material were taken by the victors in both places. Above, Greek airmen about to take off for a raid; below, a view of the harbor and town of Santi Quaranta.

AIR ATTACKS ON GREEK CIVILIANS. The Italians, in the face of the unexpectedly successful resistance of the hardy mountain troops, resorted to terror tactics in the air. The tiny Greek Air Force, magnificently as it fought, could do little to mitigate the effects of ruthless attacks on civilians. Above, an Italian photograph of a bombing raid on Yanina, the town which the Italians had unsuccessfully attempted to encircle at the beginning of their invasion. Below, shattered houses in Kastoria.

7 DECEMBER, 1940: H.M.S. "KELLY" IN SERVICE AGAIN. The British flotilla leader "Kelly" was torpedoed off the German coast in May. Badly damaged, she was towed across the North Sea to England, where she underwent repair. The first intimation of her adventure was the announcement made in December that she was again on active service. This picture, taken from another warship, shows members of her crew being transferred to another vessel.

SCUTTLED OFF CUBA. On December 8, the 5,000-ton Idarwald was intercepted off Cuba by H.M.S. Diomede. Her crew at once scuttled her, set her on fire and took to boats. A party from the British ship boarded her, fought the fire (right, below), and got it under control, but the freighter was past salvation; she soon had to be cast off and sank. Above, a boarding party from the Diomede approaches the burning ship. Right (top), the Diomede comes alongside the Idarwald as she settles in the water.

The British open an offensive against the Italians in Libya

MENACE TO EGYPT CHECKED. The lull in the Western Desert which had followed on the Italian capture of Sollum and Sidi Barrani in September was broken on December 9. At dawn on that day General Wavell's army began a general offensive. Two hours later the Italian camp at Nibeiwa, fifteen miles from Sidi Barrani, had been captured, 500 prisoners taken, and General Maletti, commander of these Italian advanced troops, killed. The attack had been preceded by a heavy bombing raid the previous night on

all the Italian airfields along the Libyan coast, seriously reducing Italy's air power in North Africa; and during the first day of the advance twenty-two Italian planes—and one British—were lost. Left, an Italian field gun put out of action and captured during the advance; the surrounding litter and dead gunner show how quickly it was abandoned. Above, a R.A.F. bomb exploding near an Italian convoy in the desert. Though most of the troops attacked have fallen flat, one machine gunner still fights on.

Italian forces driven from Sidi Barrani and Sollum

INVADERS EXPELLED FROM EGYPT. On December 11, Sidi Barrani was reoccupied, and three Italian generals, with many other prisoners, were taken. On December 16 Sollum fell again into British hands, and Egypt was freed from the invader. Anzacs and Indian troops played a great part in the victorious advance. The pictures show: above, Italian prisoners, mostly destined for internment in India, being marched away under guard of a few British soldiers; below, some of the piles of stores and equipment left behind by the enemy in their flight being loaded on to captured Italian lorries by Italian prisoners. Right, above, a gun-howitzer, protected by a dust cover from the sand, passing through Sidi Barrani; below, a signpost at Sollum pointing the way for the next British advance.

16 DECEMBER, 1940: BRITISH ENTER LIBYA. After taking over 30,000 prisoners in Egypt Wavell's victorious army crossed the border into Libya, and occupied Fort Capuzzo, south of Bardia, a frequent mark in the past for British air attacks and the first Libyan post to fall into British hands. Advance armored forces are here seen passing the Fort.

Artillery and tank units in final phase of attack on Bardia

SURROUNDING DOOMED BARDIA. The advance on Bardia by land and air forces began on 16 December. An inner circle of mobile units, supported by infantry and guns, closed up around the port, which was continually harassed by heavy artillery fire. The pictures show: top left, a howitzer, and right, artillery bombarding the town; bottom, giant tanks operating over the sandy wastes as the British forces close in.

THE GREAT FIRE
OF LONDON

DECEMBER 29, 1940

THE GREAT FIRE OF LONDON, DECEMBER 29, 1940. Christmas brought an undeclared truce in the aerial warfare over Britain, though there was some activity on the nights of December 27 and 28. On the night of the 29th came the explanation of the lull. Shortly after dark, waves of raiders, flying over the heart of the City of London, rained thousands of incendiary and explosive bombs on its historic buildings in a deliberate effort to surpass the effects of the Great Fire of 1666. St. Paul's, close-ringed by flame, remained, as by a miracle, practically unharmed; but many of Sir Christopher Wren's famous churches, the five-hundred-year-old Guildhall, banks, offices and shops by the hundred, were reduced to ashes. All through the night, watchers on the outskirts saw the great dome of St. Paul's, standing out against an awesome background of flame. Yet, throughout, the City's work went on; as the fire services, police, and civil defense workers toiled nobly at the risk of limb and life to fight the flames, and civilians helped to tackle incendiary bombs before they could start fresh fires, newspaper workers stayed at their posts, amid the conflagration, so that there should be no delay in the distribution of their papers in the morning. Not till the next day, and hardly then, could the full extent of the destruction be realized, in spite of the ferocity of the assault, and although three hospitals were hit, casualties were surprisingly few. It was made known a few days later that the attack would have been prolonged and developed still more fiercely had not the sudden development of bad weather over Northern France foiled the plans of the Luftwaffe. Realizing that much of the damage by incendiary bombs might have been avoided if they had been dealt with immediately they fell, the Government decided to make "fire-watching" compulsory and took powers to conscript all employers and employees to share, if necessary, in the protection of their places of work from fire bombs. The picture shows buildings on the river bank, with St. Paul's (right) and the slender spire of destroyed St. Bride's silhouetted against the flames at the height of the raid.

THE CITY AFTER THE RAID. It was a battered London to which workers came on the morning after the raid. Miles of hose lay tangled everywhere; firemen and auxiliaries were still pouring powerful jets on unextinguished fires, and many workers had to walk long distances before discovering whether their offices still stood. The pictures show: top, left, St. Paul's, seen through the ruined archway of a smoldering building; center, fire-fighting appliances burnt out while fighting the flames; right, firemen at work in a main City street; bottom, left, office workers climbing over hoses on their way to work; right, firemen and soldiers bring up hose.

GUILDHALL WRECKED IN FIRE RAID. The city of London's civic center, the historic Guildhall, begun in 1411 and remodelled by Sir Christopher Wren after the first Great Fire, was in large part reduced to ruins as a result of the fires which broke out when sparks and burning timbers fell on its roof from the tower of the adjoining church of St. Lawrence Jewry. The famous banqueting hall, scene of the Lord Mayor's annual banquet on November 9, is shown on the left; right, above, the entrance to the Council Chamber; below, the Lord Mayor surveying the damage.

29 DECEMBER 1940: THE DESOLATED CITY.
This picture, taken from the summit of St.
Paul's, shows one of the areas where the
Great Fire raged most fiercely. The shattered
walls to the left were Paternoster Square; Newgate Street, Paternoster Row and Warwick Lane
marked the limits of the area shown. There
had been housed business firms whose names
were known at the other end of the world.

29 DECEMBER 1940: A BLITZED CITY BACK-WATER. Here is Paternoster Square as the Germans left it. On the summit of the Old Bailey, in the background, the figure of Justice, blindfold, holds her balance and uplifted sword in the sight of the stricken City.

Historic churches destroyed in London's heaviest raid of the war

MAKING WAR ON RELIGION AND BEAUTY. The queerly-named London churches, most of which had risen under the hand of Sir Christopher Wren from the ashes of the first Great Fire in 1666, suffered heavily in the second conflagration of 1940. Above, left, the interior of St. Bride's, Fleet Street, the church of newspaperland, famous for its slender spire, one of Wren's masterpieces; center, the ruins of St. Mary the Virgin, Aldermanbury, where Shakespeare once habitually worshipped; right, All Hallows, Barking, famous in all English-speaking lands as the headquarters of Toc H: in the background is the "Crusaders' Chapel," with its destroyed altar. Below, left, all that was left of St. Giles', Cripplegate, the burial place of Milton, John Foxe, and the Elizabethan sailor, Martin Frobisher; this church, like All Hallows, Barking, survived the first Great Fire only to perish in the second. Center, the ruins of Christchurch, Greyfriars, Newgate Street, where the "Bluecoat Boys" of Christ's Hospital held their annual commemorative service. Right, charred debris within the battered walls of the church of St. Andrew by the Wardrobe. Other churches seriously damaged include St. Lawrence Jewry, the "official" church of the City Corporation; St. Stephen and St. Mary Woolnoth.

5 JANUARY 1941: BRITISH TAKE BARDIA.
The capture of Bardia was finally effected after
an assault of less than four days: 38,000 prisoners,
including four generals, and vast quantities of
material, were taken with the town. Above, Australian troops advancing into Bardia; below, Italian prisoners taken at Bardia marching past Sollum.

The Nazi raiders take their toll in Plymouth and Portsmouth

SOUTH COAST NAVAL BASES RAIDED. Intense night air attacks were made on Portsmouth on January 10 and on Plymouth three days later. Churches, hospitals and private dwellings were damaged in each case and many persons rendered homeless. Left, top, the remains of St. Andrew's, Plymouth's mother church. Bottom, weary firemen at Plymouth, after fighting the flames all night, run up the Union Jack on a lamp-post. Above, the funeral of some of the Portsmouth victims: twenty-five bodies in a common grave.

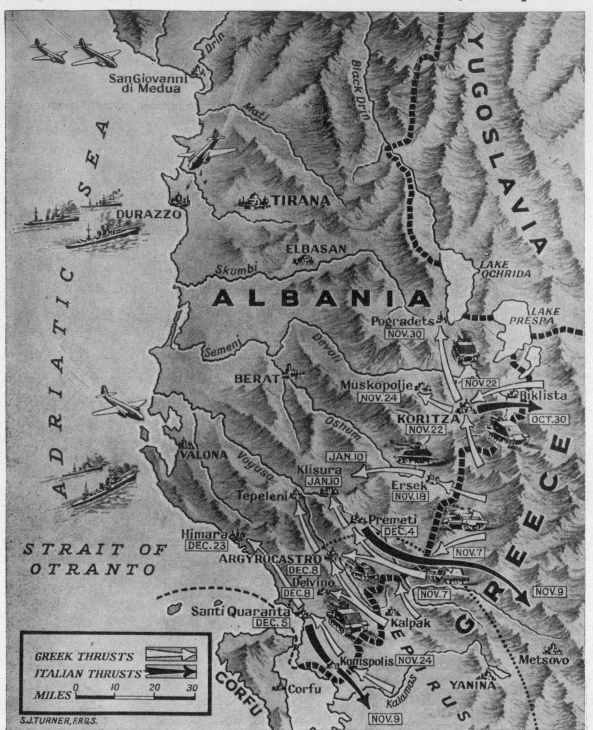

ALBANIAN CAMPAIGN. The map above shows the direction of the early Italian thrust into northern Greece which reached its "farthest south" on November 9, after crossing the Kalamas and, farther east, striking at Metsovo through the Sarandoporo valley. Here the crack Italian "Venezia Alpini" were cut off and isolated by the Greeks, who then became the attackers, first in the north-east towards Koritza and Pogradets, then in the center towards Premeti and Klisura and finally along the coast in the direction of Santi Quaranta and Himara.

A FIRST HAND VIEW OF THE WAR. Wendell Willkie arrived in England in January. He conferred with Winston Churchill and other English leaders, visited defense plants and inspected bomb damage in London and the provinces, and reiterated his determination to do everything possible to aid Britain in America. Above, he is seen (right foreground) visiting a shelter during an air raid; below, enthusiastic crowds greet him as he leaves his automobile during a visit to Manchester.

21 JANUARY 1941: ITALIAN CRUISER FIRED IN TOBRUK HARBOR. The cruiser "San Giorgio," damaged earlier in the month by the R.A.F. and beached in Tobruk Harbor, where she was used as a fortress mounting anti-aircraft guns, was set on fire from the air on 21 January. The picture shows her last moments as she burns furiously amidships.

Infantry and mechanized forces combine to capture Tobruk

ASSAULT ON TOBRUK. The battle of Tobruk followed the lines of that at Bardia, the town being attacked simultaneously from several points. By skilfully encircling the enemy positions the attackers were able to take Italian forces in the rear, thereby throwing them into confusion and making them face both ways at once. Allied casualties were very light, less than 500 in all; nearly 20,000 Italian prisoners were taken as

well as many guns and large stores of material. Above, left, a British medium howitzer in action during the preliminary bombardment. Right, British infantry making their way through barbed wire defenses outside the town. Below, men of the Australian Imperial forces advancing towards their objective supported by light tanks. They are disposed in open formation as a precaution against bombing from the air.

HAILE SELASSIE AT HOME AGAIN. The British successes against the Italians in Abyssinia encouraged the Ethiopians to revolt. When Ras Mongasha raised the Imperial standard at Gojjam in July, 1940, large numbers of the patriots rallied to the call. A British mission had kept in close contact with the patriots, and the Emperor, Haile Selassie, established in Kahrtum, had visited his troops at the frontier at the end of the previous year. On January 15 he flew into the heart of Abyssinia, where he unfurled his standard (above) on his native soil. In the lower picture he is seen stepping from his plane at a secret field.

President Roosevelt's welcome to Lord Halifax January 24, 1941

NEW BRITISH AMBASSADOR IN AMERICA. The death of Lord Lothian, Britain's representative, in Washington, on December 12, 1940, left a diplomatic gap which was filled a fortnight later by the appointment of Lord Halifax. The selection of so prominent a statesman as Ambassador was unprecedented, and was received with deep satisfaction in the United States. Lord Halifax, who crossed to America in the battleship King George V, was met in Chesapeake Bay by President Roosevelt, who had journeyed from Washington to welcome him. Above, the President and the new Ambassador together shortly after the latter's arrival.

JANUARY 29, 1941: DERNA CAPTURED. Derna, the next objective on the Libyan coast after Tobruk for General Wavell's troops, was captured by the Australians and British on January 29 after three days' fighting. Though their strength had been sapped at Bardia and Tobruk, the Italians defended this vital water depot with great tenacity. The picture shows British artillery pounding at the defenses of the town.

FALL OF AGORDAT. On February 1, the Anglo-Indian forces, with R.A.F. support, captured Agordat, capital of Western Eritrea. The enemy suffered heavy casualties and lost a number of tanks and guns. This success cleared the road to Keren, on which town was based the defense of Asmara, the Eritrean capital, and the Red Sea port of Massawa. The pictures show, above, Indians with a Bren gun carrier clearing an Eritrean village, below, British soldiers with Bren guns and rifles sniping from behind the rocks.

CAPITAL OF EASTERN LIBYA OCCUPIED. The Army of the Nile crowned its two months' campaign on February 6 by occupying Benghazi, capital of Eastern Libya. The resistance encountered here was small, for after a British mechanized force had cut the town's communications in the south, the enemy surrendered without a fight. Above, Italian and native residents watch the ceremony of handing over the town to the victors: below, inhabitants give the Australian troops a warm welcome as they march into town.

The campaign in Libya—stages of the British advance

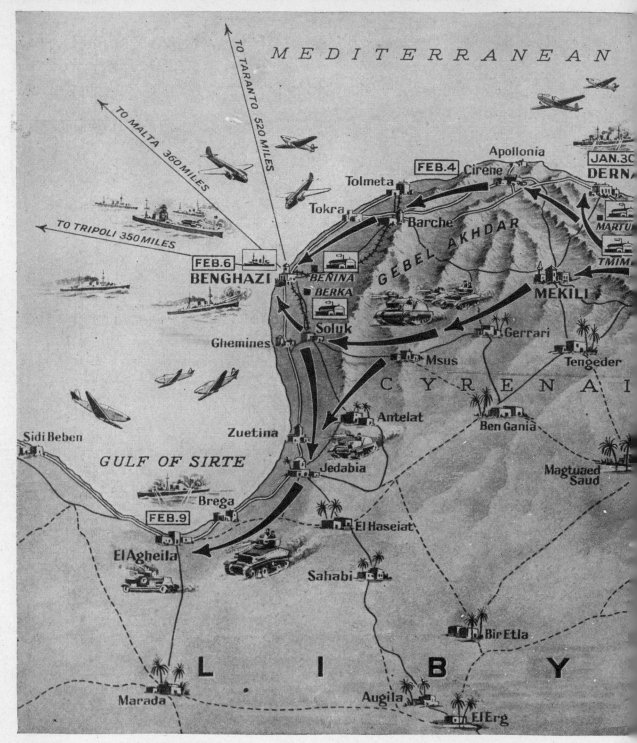

BRITAIN'S CONQUEST OF EASTERN LIBYA. The brilliant forward movement along the coast of Italian North Africa, begun on December 9, 1940, and culminating in the capture of Benghazi on February 6, 1941, was acclaimed as one of the most brilliant campaigns in military history. The army of the Nile, consisting of about 30,000 men, advanced within two months over 500 miles through practically roadless and waterless country, with ever-lengthening lines of communication. They captured about 140,000 prisoners, including

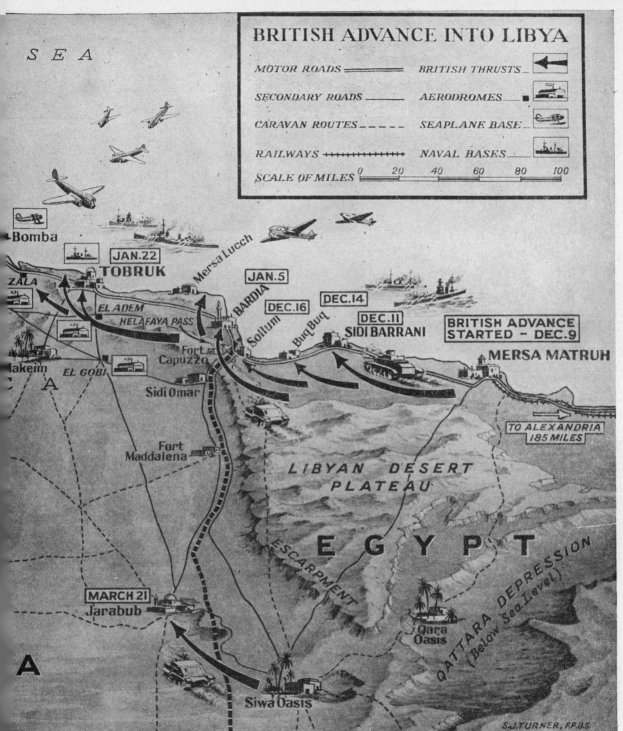

BRITISH ADVANCE INTO LIBYA

MOTOR ROADS	BRITISH THRUSTS
SECONDARY ROADS	AERODROMES
CARAVAN ROUTES	SEAPLANE BASE
RAILWAYS	NAVAL BASES
SCALE OF MILES 0 20 40 60 80 100	

SEA

Bomba

JAN.22 TOBRUK

Mersa Lucch

ZALA

EL ADEM
HELAFAYA PASS

JAN.5

BARDIA

DEC.16

Sollum

DEC.14

DEC.11
SIDI BARRANI

BuqBuq

BRITISH ADVANCE
STARTED - DEC.9

MERSA MATRUH

Fort
Capuzzo

akeim

EL GOBI

Sidi Omar

TO ALEXANDRIA
185 MILES

Fort
Maddalena

LIBYAN DESERT
PLATEAU

E G Y P T

ESCARPMENT

QATTARA DEPRESSION
(Below Sea Level)

MARCH 21
Jarabub

Qara
Oasis

A

Siwa Oasis

S.J.TURNER, F.R.G.S.

nineteen enemy generals, with vast quantities of war material of all kinds, at a cost of only about 2,000 British casualties. During the earlier stages great assistance was given to the land army by naval supporting forces, and the success was also due in great measure to the air superiority early established by the R.A.F. The map above shows pictorially the stages of the advance, indicating the final move on Benghazi by Australian troops using the coastal road and British armored units cutting Italian communications from the south.

ROYAL NAVY POUNDS ITALIAN NAVAL BASE. In an early morning bombardment of Genoa by the Mediterranean Fleet on February 9 more than three hundred tons of shells were rained on the harbor. Many important objectives, including the main power station, the Ansaldo electrical and boiler works, the oil fuel installations, and several supply ships, were repeatedly hit by heavy shells. Above, a view of the harbor at Genoa; below, the battleship Renown, which took part in the bombardment, carrying out gunnery practice.

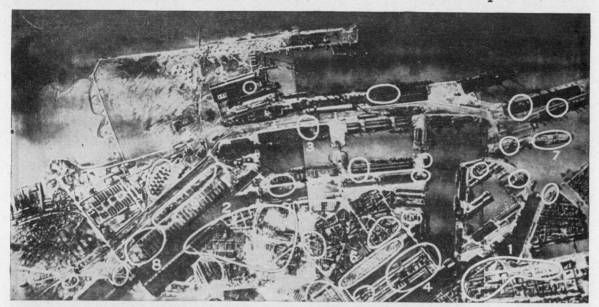

INVASION POINTS ATTACKED. During the winter the R.A.F. attacks on the "invasion ports" continued, and, with the approach of Spring were redoubled. The accuracy of the British bombings is well illustrated by the above photographs taken by reconnaissance planes shortly afterwards. They show (above), damage at LeHavre: No. 1, Kleber Barracks, Numbers 2 to 8, partially or completely destroyed warehouses and other buildings on the docks. No. 9, sheds by the Harbor Railway Station, and below, the docks at Ostend.

BRITAIN'S AIRBORNE TROOPS. On the night of February 10, British parachute detachments landed in Calabria, South Italy, to demolish port objectives in the neighborhood. The training of the new arm was undertaken by the army and the R.A.F. at a secret station in Great Britain. On the left are seen some of the parachutists in the second stage of their training. They are jumping from a dummy fuselage, counter-balance weights regulate the speed of their fall, making it equivalent to that which would be attained in an actual jump. Above, troops are jumping from their planes and, below, the descent as the parachutes open.

South African troops push on in Italian Somaliland

THE CAPITAL FALLS. The South African and Gold Coast troops advancing into Italian Somaliland occupied on February 11 the military center of Afmadu, and on the 15th captured the port of Kismayu, the British fleet co-operating with the attackers. Jumbo was taken on the 23rd and the way opened to the capital, Mogadishu, which fell on the 25th. Some of the Italian native troops who were taken prisoner are shown above, left: top right, a British doctor examines a wounded prisoner. Below, left, some of the guns and equipment captured from the Italians; right, inhabitants of Mogadishu, under the shadow of the fasces, watch with interest naval vessels off the capital.

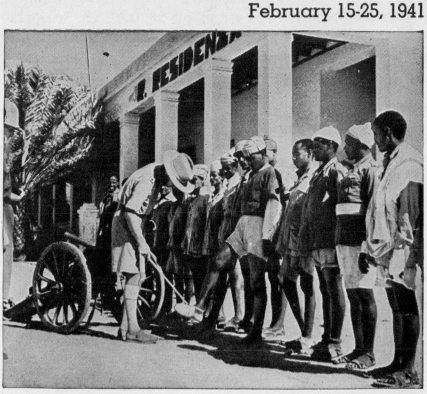

The distaff side plays a big part in Britain's war effort

THE WOMEN GO TO IT. As the armed forces and war industries absorbed additional men, more and more women came forward to fill their places. Top left, a girl mechanic is at work on machine gun parts;

center, women training to be bus conductors; right, women porters at a railway yard; bottom, left, Britain's first women signalers learning the job; right, girls loading a mail train at a London terminus.

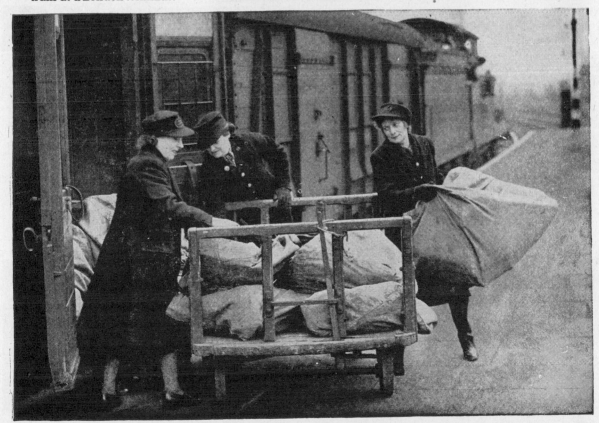

Bulgaria joins the Axis—Sofia occupied by the Nazis

BULGARIA ACCEPTS "NEW ORDER." Bulgaria had frequently reiterated her intention of maintaining neutrality, but at the end of February it became obvious that the pretense was wearing thin, and on March 1 the Premier, Prof. Filoff, flew to Vienna and there (top right) signed a pact with the Axis in Hitler's presence. Filoff is seated left, with Ribbentrop (centre) and Count Ciano (right). Top, left, German Stuka dive bombers flying over Sofia, as hints that quick signature would be advisable; below, left, German tanks enter Bulgaria, which the Nazis had already begun to occupy as the pact was being signed; right, Nazi tanks in Sofia.

NEW ENVOY TO THE COURT OF ST. JAMES'S. On February 10 it was announced that John G. Winant would succeed Joseph P. Kennedy as American ambassador to the Court of St. James's. Mr. Winant arrived in England on March 1 and was welcomed to London (above) by the King. Below, seated, left to right, Lord Moyne, Colonial Secretary; Lord Cranborne, Dominions Secretary; Mr. Winant and Winston Churchill, signing the agreement providing for the lease of air and naval bases in British possessions to America.

LOFOTEN ISLANDS RAIDED. On March 4, British troops and light naval forces, aided by Norwegian marines, carried out a raid on the Lofoten Islands, near Narvik. They destroyed the fish-oil production plant, sank eleven enemy ships, took a number of prisoners, brought off about 300 Norwegian patriots, and left supplies for the civilians. Little opposition was encountered and no casualties suffered. The picture shows a motor landing craft with troops aboard, making for the shore to effect the landing.

4 MARCH, 1941: **GERMAN OIL PLANT DESTROYED.** Here the oil storage wells at Stansund are seen ablaze after they have been fired by the landing party. The British troops in the foreground are guarding the wells while their comrades round up the "Quislings" and German personnel.

Raiders capture "Quislings" and leave oil tanks ablaze

RESULTS OF THE LOFOTEN RAID. The raid on the Lofotens took the Nazis completely by surprise. The attackers met with practically no opposition, and suffered no casualties, though a few German sailors were killed. Above, German merchant seamen and air ground staff and Norwegian "quislings" being transferred, blindfolded, from one ship to another on the way to Britain; below, one of the landing craft leaving after the raid loaded with troops and recruits for the Free Norwegian forces; top, right, British troops return to their ship, leaving smoking oil tanks behind; below, dense clouds of smoke rising from the burning oil tanks.

MORE AMERICAN AID. On January 10, President Roosevelt introduced in Congress a Lend-Lease bill, providing for authority to be given to the United States to manufacture defense articles of all kinds and to "sell, lease, lend or otherwise dispose of" them to the Allied governments. After hot debates in Congress the bill became law on March 11. Above, Wendell Willkie urging passage of the bill before the Senate Foreign Relations Committee: below, Mr. Roosevelt signing the bill at the White House as cameras grind.

THE A.T.S. ON THE JOB. The auxiliary territorial service, formed some months prior to the war, was now performing duties of the first importance in connection with home defense, especially in anti-aircraft operations. Above A.T.S. girls at a training post for anti-aircraft gunners; while the gunners fire at a target, the girls on the left photograph the shell-bursts with a kine-theodolite, while those at the table map the hits: below, women in battle dress rush to action stations at an A.A. post where they operate predictors.

Clydeside and Merseyside heavily bombed by the Luftwaffe

NAZI BOMBERS OVER THE PROVINCES. The main attack of the Luftwaffe was now being directed against the large industrial cities of the provinces, especially the ports and coastal towns. Heavy raids on Merseyside took place on March 12 and 13, the damage being mainly confined to private houses, though schools, a hospital, and industrial premises were also hit. The first heavy attack on Clydeside came on March 13 and

was resumed on the following night, blocks of flats and tenement houses being the chief sufferers. Thirteen enemy bombers—record number so far—were destroyed on the night of March 13. Left, bombed-out Clyde-siders take their rescued belongings to temporary shelter; right, above, homeless women and children in a Liverpool street after a night raid; below, Merseyside rescue workers searching the wreckage for victims.

U. S. warships visit Australia and New Zealand

U.S. SQUADRON AT SYDNEY. In March a U.S. naval squadron comprising two cruisers and five destroyers paid a visit to Australia and New Zealand. It was commanded by Admiral Newton who, at a dinner given by the Commonwealth Government to himself and his officers, declared that the U.S. was behind Britain and her dominions in their great fight for freedom. American sailors and marines who marched through Sydney

followed by detachments of militia and the Royal Australian Air Force, received a tremendous welcome from the people of the city. The previous visit by U.S. warships to Australian waters had been made in June, 1926. The picture above shows launches escorting the American warships down Sydney harbor. Less than nine months later American forces were to be stationed in Australia under General MacArthur.

Devastation in Plymouth after heavy night raids

LADY ASTOR'S CONSTITUENCY HIT. Nazi bombers made Plymouth their main target in two particularly heavy night raids towards the end of March. The destruction wrought by the attacks was officially stated to be at least as heavy as any provincial city had so far sustained in air attacks. The "military objectives" hit included dwellings, shops, churches, film houses and hotels, and the casualties were heavy. In the second raid, the more severe of the two, more than 20,000 incendiary bombs were dropped, in addition to hundreds

of high explosives. These were followed by sustained dive bombing and machine gun attacks on the ruins, but on both nights serious fires were soon brought under control by the local fire-fighting services who stayed at their posts in spite of the ferocity of the bombardment. Mr. Menzies, the Australian premier, who was in the city at the time, helped in the rescue work. Left, one of the bombed areas of a business district; right, Prime Minister Churchill is welcomed by workmen as he tours the city after the raids.

Jarabub surrenders after a siege of fifteen weeks

ITALIAN DESERT GARRISON CAPTURED. Jarabub, an isolated town in the Libyan desert, about 250 miles south of Tobruk, and the burial place of the founder of the Senussi sect of Mohammedans, was captured by British and Imperial troops on March 21 after a siege lasting fifteen weeks. The pictures show: top, left,

Australians with fixed bayonets searching the citadel for Italian troops who may be in hiding; below, left, the inhabitants watching an Australian battalion parading for roll call after the battle; right, Australian soldiers beside the bodies of two of the many Italian soldiers who perished during the final assualt.

Germans come to the aid of their ally in Libya

NAZIS TO ITALY'S AID. The farthest point on the Libyan coast reached by Wavell's army was El Agheila, 175 miles west of Benghazi. On March 24 it was announced that this small town had been re-occupied by an enemy force believed to include German armored units. It later transpired that the Germans had succeeded in shipping panzer units to Africa to bolster the morale of the Italians. Above, German soldiers are unloading guns from a transport plane and, below, a German Stork plane, just landed from a transport.

KEREN FALLS TO THE BRITISH. Keren, Italian key fortress in Eritrea, defended by some 60,000 men, a third of the Italian forces in East Africa, fell to the British on March 26. In the capture of the heights over-looking the town Indian troops, fighting against tremendous odds, played a magnificent part. The pictures show, top, airmen who took part in the bombing of the town being shown their objectives on a scale model of the battle area; below, an Indian observation post on one of the mountains close to the town.

GERMAN PLAN FOR BALKANS FOILED. In mid-March Germany demanded that Yugoslavia should align itself with the Axis powers, and on the 25th the Premier, M. Tsvetkovich, signed at Vienna a treaty by which Yugoslavia adhered to the Tripartite Pact. The news was received with consternation in the country, and at midnight on the 26th a revolution broke out, led by General Simovich, who became Premier. Above, M. Tsvetkovich (center) and his foreign minister, M. Cincar-Markovich (left) take leave of Ribbentrop at Salzburg after a conference with Hitler in February; below, students demonstrating in a Belgrade street after the coup.

FATE OF GERMAN U-BOATS. With the approach of spring the Nazi campaign against British and Allied shipping was greatly intensified, and in March the total losses, British, Allied, and neutral, amounted to 119 ships, with a total tonnage of 489,229 tons. German battle cruisers as well as U-boats were reported to be operating in the Atlantic, but measures against the raiders were intensified too, and the certain destruction of three U-boats was announced during the month. Upper picture shows the last member of a destroyed U-boat's crew about to jump from the vessel; below, the crew in the water after abandoning ship.

ITALY'S CRUSHING DEFEAT. On March 28 reconnaissance planes reported the presence of the Italian battleship Vittorio Veneto with eight cruisers and nine destroyers off Sicily. The Mediterranean Fleet immediately put to sea and joined action. During the day-and-night-long engagement three of Italy's heaviest cruisers, the Pola, the Fiume and the Zara as well as two large destroyers were sunk. The above pictures show aspects of the first stage of the battle: top, H.M. destroyer Hasty steaming past enemy shells bursting near her; center, destroyers laying a smoke screen to protect British ships from the fire of the Italian battleship, Vittorio Veneto, which was later damaged; bottom, H.M.S. Gloucester laying a smoke screen.

GERMANS BOMB ITALIAN SAILORS. It was estimated that 3,000 Italian officers and men, including an admiral, perished in the Matapan engagement. British ships picked up more than 900 survivors as well as thirty-five German naval officers and men, and the number of men so rescued would have been much larger had not German dive bombing attacks compelled the rescue work to be abandoned. Admiral Cunningham, the British commander, then signalled the position of the unrescued Italians to their own authorities so that a hospital ship could be sent. The picture above shows three rafts with Italian sailors waiting to be rescued.

How the Nazis tried to strangle Britain's lifeline

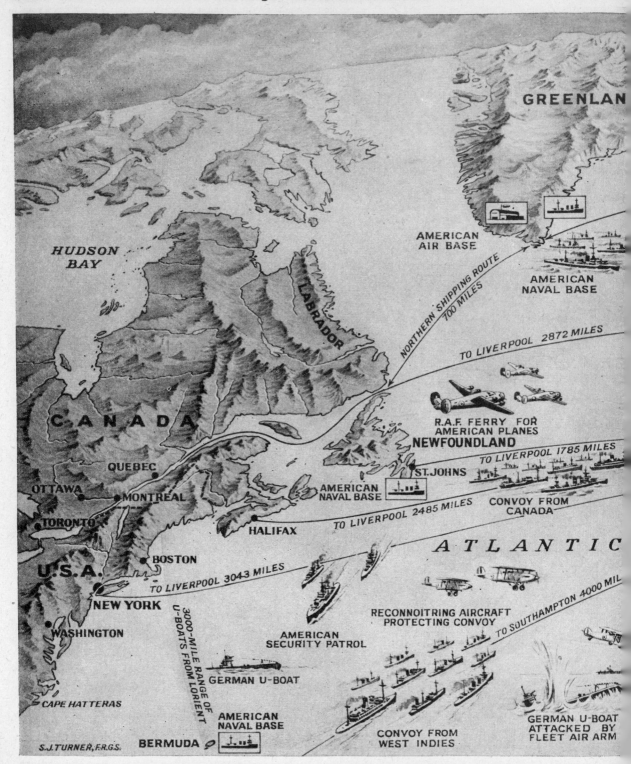

GREENLAN[D]

HUDSON BAY

LABRADOR

AMERICAN AIR BASE

AMERICAN NAVAL BASE

NORTHERN SHIPPING ROUTE 700 MILES

TO LIVERPOOL 2872 MILES

R.A.F. FERRY FOR AMERICAN PLANES

CANADA

NEWFOUNDLAND

TO LIVERPOOL 1785 MILES

QUEBEC

ST. JOHNS

AMERICAN NAVAL BASE

CONVOY FROM CANADA

OTTAWA

MONTREAL

TORONTO

TO LIVERPOOL 2485 MILES

HALIFAX

ATLANTIC

U.S.A.

BOSTON

TO LIVERPOOL 3043 MILES

NEW YORK

3000-MILE RANGE OF U-BOATS FROM LORIENT

RECONNOITRING AIRCRAFT PROTECTING CONVOY

TO SOUTHAMPTON 4000 MIL[ES]

WASHINGTON

AMERICAN SECURITY PATROL

GERMAN U-BOAT

AMERICAN NAVAL BASE

CAPE HATTERAS

BERMUDA

CONVOY FROM WEST INDIES

GERMAN U-BOAT ATTACKED BY FLEET AIR ARM

S.J.TURNER, F.R.G.S.

BATTLE OF THE ATLANTIC. Hitler's boast, that with the coming of Spring, German U-boat and aerial war against Britain's convoys in the Atlantic would be intensified was no idle one. In March and April British and Allied losses rose to 489,229 tons respectively, representing in all 225 ships. In spite of all the enemy

GERMAN AEROPLANE BASE

GERMAN SUBMARINE BASE

SCORESBY SOUND

DENMARK STRAIT

AMERICAN NAVAL BASE

ICELAND

600 MILES

FAROE IS.

GERMAN BOMBER ATTACKED BY R.A.F.

NARVIK

HAMMERFEST

TRONDHJEM

1000-MILE RANGE OF GERMAN BOMBERS FROM STAVANGER

CONVOY FROM CANADA

DANGEROUS AREA OF WESTERN APPROACHES

BRITISH ISLES

EIRE

LIVERPOOL

HULL

EDINBURGH

SHETLAND IS.

BERGEN

ORKNEY IS.

STAVANGER

NORTH SEA

DENMARK

600 MILES

TRAFFIC LANES PATROLLED BY COASTAL COMMAND

TRAFFIC LANES PATROLLED BY COASTAL COMMAND

LONDON

BRITAIN'S LIFE LINES

SOUTHAMPTON

CHERBOURG

HAVRE

PARIS

BREST

LORIENT

BOULOGNE

HAMBURG

BERLIN

GERMANY

CONVOY FROM AMERICA

CONVOY ATTACKED BY GERMAN BOMBERS

BAY OF BISCAY

VICHY

MERIGNAC

OCEAN

1000-MILE RANGE OF GERMAN BOMBERS FROM MERIGNAC

BARCELONA

AZORES

TO SOUTHAMPTON 3875 MILES

LISBON

PORTUGAL

SPAIN

MADRID

MEDITERRANEAN

FROM CAPE TOWN 5917 MILES

CADIZ

GIBRALTAR

ALGIERS

TANGIER

CONVOY FROM BRITISH GUIANA

MADEIRA

RABAT

SPANISH MOROCCO

MOROCCO (FRENCH)

ALGERIA (FRENCH)

could do, however, Britain's lifeline, although stretched, remained unbroken due to the efforts of the British fleet and the R.A.F. The map above shows the routes taken by convoys from America and Canada and measures taken to outwit enemy submarines and long-range bombers.

HEROES OF THE BATTLE OF THE ATLANTIC. As Hitler had threatened, Nazi efforts to cut Britain's lifeline reached their climax in the spring. In spite of heavy losses from U-boats and surface raiders, food and munitions still poured into Britain. The pictures show: top, fast motor launches guarding a convoy as it steams down the English Channel; below, the look-out of a destroyer scans the sea for possible enemy submarines.

MEN WHO COMMAND THE U-BOATS. The British announced in May that, although many U-Boats had been destroyed leaving no survivors, about 500 officers and men from sunken submarines had been made prisoners. Among them was Commander Otto Kretschmer, U-Boat ace, decorated by Hitler in August, 1940. Another noted commander, Captain Schepke, went down with his boat in mid-April. The picture above shows Captain Schutze, another Nazi hero, saying farewell before leaving for a raiding cruise.

THE FALL OF ASMARA. On April 1, British forces advancing after their victory at Keren accepted the surrender of Asmara, capital of Italy's oldest colony, a city of 100,000 persons. It had been declared an open town by the Italians, and the defending forces withdrew to new positions to the south of the city. The upper picture shows Imperial troops and Bren gun carriers marching through the city; below, some of the Indian troops who had played such a great and gallant part in the advance are seen entering the town.

ALLIED LEADERS IN THE MIDDLE EAST. The resumption of activity in Libya brought about by German reinforcements created a difficult situation for the middle eastern command, for the expected attack on Greece made it imperative that troops should be withdrawn from the African front. As a result British and Free French commanders met in Cairo to discuss the situation. Above they are in conversation. Left to right, **General Catroux, General Wavell, General de Gaulle, General Spears and Air Marshal Longmire.**

NAZIS ADVANCE IN LIBYA. The withdrawal of large numbers of British troops from Cyrenaica enabled the German division that had come to Italy's aid in the previous month to push the slender British forces back. On April 3 the enemy entered Benghazi, but the British were able to destroy all the war material they had previously captured from the Italians. The pictures show the advance of a Nazi panzer division along the coastal road in Cyrenaica. The natives in the lower picture appear to be accustomed to the sight of tanks.

MERCHANT SHIPS SCUTTLED IN AMERICA. After acts of sabotage by the crews of Italian merchant ships in American ports, the government decided to place Axis vessels in "protective custody." This example was followed a few days later by other American republics. When the Italian steamship Fella (top, left) and the German Eisenach (top right) were set on fire at Puntarenas, the Costa Rica government charged their crews with arson. Below, seamen from the Conte Biancamano being taken into custody at Ellis Island.

South African troops enter Addis Ababa in triumph

ABYSSINIAN CAPITAL RECOVERED. On the evening of April 5, South African troops, after an advance of 700 miles in the short space of twenty-seven days, entered Addis Ababa, thus wrested from Italian hands after an occupation lasting since 1936. The city was surrendered by the Italians without any attempt at resistance; the Italian Viceroy, the Duke of Aosta, and part of the garrison had already withdrawn. In the pic-

ture a well-known Transvaal regiment, headed by its pipers, is seen marching through the liberated town accompanied by delighted Abyssinians who after five years under the Fascist yoke, have been freed from virtual slavery. A month later, on May 5, the fifth anniversary of the entry of the Italian troops into the capital, Emperor Haile Selassie returned in triumph and was greeted by all his religious and military leaders.

417

An angry Germany moves her troops into Yugoslavia

ANOTHER VICTIM OF NAZI AGGRESSION. Germany's anger at the coup d'etat which had spoiled her plans in Yugoslavia at once reached fever pitch. A campaign of abuse began in the German press, "atrocities" against German residents in Yugoslavia were alleged, and German consular officials were called home. On April 6, without declaration of war or previous warning, Germany invaded Yugoslavia and Greece. Aid from Britain and America to the invaded countries was immediately promised, but the new Government in Belgrade had had no time to make preparations against attack, and the country was quickly overrun. The pictures show: top, left, tank traps being pushed aside by German tanks during the march in; right, uprooted rail tracks after a bombing raid; below, left, Yugoslav infantrymen waiting for the invader; right, light tanks and motor cycle combinations of a German "panzer" division moving into Yugoslavia.

Belgrade bombed and occupied by the Nazi hordes

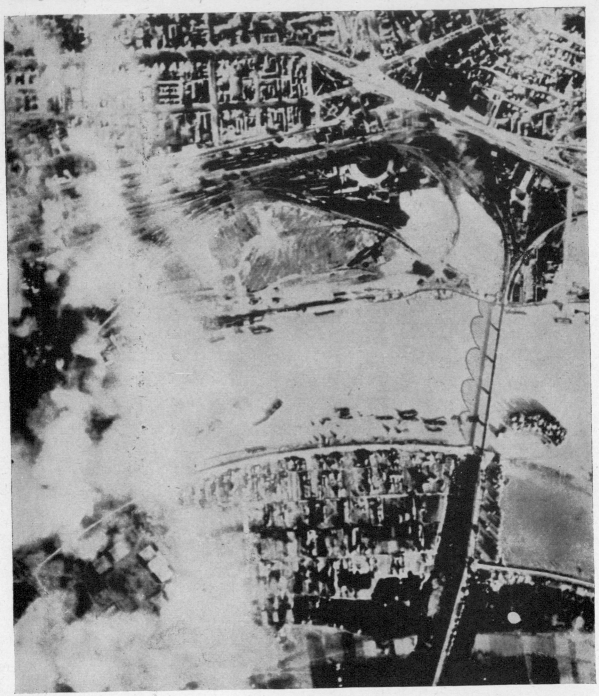

RUTHLESS ATTACK ON YUGOSLAV CAPITAL. The German onslaught on Yugoslavia opened with a savage bombing raid on Belgrade in the morning of April 6, in spite of the fact that the capital had been declared an open city. Three further attacks took place during the day, rivalling in ferocity the earlier raids on Warsaw and Rotterdam. Although the small Yugoslav air force gallantly attacked the numerically superior enemy formations, thousands of civilians were killed, and much of the city laid in ruins. Above, an aerial view of part of the city just after the first raid, showing fires raging in several quarters. Right, Nazi tanks passing General von Kleist in front of the Parliament after the occupation of the city on April 12.

Drive on the Balkans—German columns advance on Greece

FIRST DAY OF BALKAN ADVANCE. Germany began the attack on Greece by an advance through the Rupel Pass into the Struma Valley, leading from Bulgaria into Greece, with a view to the capture of Salonika and the cutting off of the Greek troops in eastern Thrace from their main body. The pictures show various aspects of the advance: top, left, a Nazi motorized unit protected by anti-aircraft guns against surprise at-

tack from the air, pressing on through the rough Balkan countryside on their way to the Greek frontier; below, German artillerymen hauling an 8-8 cm. gun across a pontoon bridge hastily erected over a Balkan river; right, a German tank ablaze after it received a direct hit from Greek artillery. The trailer ropes at the left of the picture show that it was aiding another damaged vehicle when it was itself destroyed.

THE NAZIS ROLL ON. German armored divisions captured Dedeagach on April 7, thus cutting off Greece from Turkey, and on the following day the rapid advance down the Vardar Valley after the Yugoslavs had withdrawn from southern Serbia enabled the Nazis to occupy Salonika. Greek and British troops had destroyed the port installations before the German occupation. The picture shows German anti-tank gunners who took part in the Balkan operations in action against the Greek mechanized units.

Berlin gets a taste of its own medicine

BOMB DAMAGE IN GERMAN CAPITAL. On the night of April 9 British airmen made the heaviest attack on Berlin which the city had so far suffered. Neutral reports said that terrific damage was done, especially in the Government quarter and that civilian casualties amounted to more than 2,000. The State Opera House, from which flames are seen pouring in the picture above, Prussian State Library, Bellevue Palace, and the New Palace at Potsdam, suffered severely from the effects of the heavy high-explosive bombs.

HUNGARIANS BREAK TREATY OF FRIENDSHIP. In February Hungary signed a pact of eternal friendship with Yugoslavia: the lower picture shows the Hungarian and Yugoslav Foreign Ministers, MM. Bardossy (left) and Cincar-Markovich (centre) reviewing a guard of honor on this occasion in Budapest. But on April 11 Hungarian troops invaded the Banat, which had been Hungarian territory before 1918. In the upper picture a brigade of Hungarian motorized troops that took part in the invasion is passing through Budapest.

INTENSE AIR ATTACK ON CAPITAL. On the night of April 16 a force of more than 500 German bombers attacked London in what was estimated to be its most destructive raid of the war up to that date. Most of the damage done was by fire, the Nazis claiming that more than 100,000 incendiary bombs were dropped. Hospitals, churches, private residences and other non-military objectives suffered most severely. This photograph of a blazing building in the heart of the city was taken at the height of the blitz.

Churches in London and other cities destroyed in April raids

HEAVY NIGHT RAIDS DE-STROY MORE CHURCHES. Churches were among the principal sufferers in the heavy raid on London of April 16, and the almost equally heavy raid three nights later. These raids were announced in Germany as reprisals for the successful R.A.F. raid on Berlin on the night of April 9-10. In the attack of the 16th, six enemy bombers were shot down—three by A.A. fire and three by night-fighters, bringing the month's total to sixty-five and the year's to 142. Wide-spread raids over provincial towns also took place during April, especially at Belfast on the 15th and Portsmouth on the 17th. The pictures show: top, left, St. Mildred's, Bread Street, London, a Wren church which has been called "a miniature Essay for St. Paul's"; centre,

a Belfast Presbyterian church; right, the gutted shell of St. Clement Danes, one of Wren's greatest creations, its charred and bare walls still standing on its island site in the Strand roadway. This famous church had been damaged in previous raids. Bottom, left, the results of a further hit on St. Paul's Cathedral, where a gaping hole in the floor of the north transept was caused by a bomb falling through the roof. Several incendiary bombs fell on to the roof but were quickly extinguished. Centre, the rubble where once stood the seven-hundred-year-old parish church of Bromley, Kent, destroyed, save for its tower, by a direct hit; right, what the Nazis left of the Catholic Cathedral of St. George, Southwark. Several other buildings were damaged in the raid of the 16th.

YUGOSLAVIA FALLS. Although the Yugoslav troops put up a brave resistance to the invaders, their position was hopeless from the beginning, for the government that had been in power before the coup d'etat on March 27 had done nothing to prepare the country for the struggle. On April 16 Sarajevo was captured and the Yugoslav army capitulated on April 17. The upper picture shows Yugoslav troops with the white flag of surrender after the capitulation, marching under escort down a road lined with German tanks; below, a blockhouse fired by defenders when further resistance was impossible, is occupied by German troops.

ARMY OF EPIRUS HARD PRESSED. The occupation of Yugoslavia and the consequent release of German troops rendered critical the position of the Greek armies that had gallantly harried the Italians in southern Albania. A strongly mechanized German thrust to their rear near Yanina soon cut them off from the main Greek army farther south; their anti-tank equipment was negligible, and in spite of the desperate resistance of small isolated groups such as that shown in the lower picture, they failed to stem the German advance. Above, Nazi troops, covered by machine gunners, are operating against the Greeks with flame-throwers.

German armies join forces with the Italians in Albania

EPIRUS FORCES SURROUNDED. The German advance from Monastir, besides separating the Greeks in Epirus from their comrades to the south, enabled the German and Italian troops to join forces. The picture

shows an Italian artilleryman firing a medium gun at the crumbling Greek concentrations behind the front line in Albania shortly before the Greek Army was forced to surrender to the combined Axis forces.

END OF A BRAVE STRUGGLE. The Greek army of Epirus and Macedonia surrendered at Larissa on the afternoon of April 22, after a heroic fight against greatly superior German and Italian forces, and signed an armistice with the Italian commander; on the same day the Greek king and government left the mainland for Crete. Top, General Tsolakoglu signs the armistice documents placed before him by German staff officers; below, Greek soldiers of the Epirot army with an out-of-date field-piece, typical of the weapons with which they had for so long held the Italians, but which availed little against the superior equipment of the Nazis.

GERMANS ATTACK DESERT GARRISON. Although the British were obliged to abandon most of the territory they had captured in Libya, they managed to hold the strategically important town of Tobruk. Supplied with food and munitions by sea, the garrison beat off repeated enemy attacks in one of which, on April 25, they captured two officers and 125 men, besides killing and wounding many others. These pictures, taken inside the Tobruk defenses, show, above, an A.A. gun team, behind a barricade of munition boxes, on the watch for Nazi bombers; below, a British transport unloading food and munitions for the defenders.

German troops occupy Corinth and Greek islands

NAZIS TIGHTEN THEIR GRIP ON GREECE. The Anglo-Greek forces were compelled to fall back as heavy reinforcements of German troops and equipment supported by dive bombers in vast numbers, poured into northern Greece. Whole regiments of Germans were cut down in rearguard actions as the British and Greeks withdrew to shorter defense lines. On April 25, the famous pass of Thermopylae was taken after

heroic resistance by Anzac troops; on the same day German troops occupied Lamnos and other Greek islands; on April 26 they took Thebes and on the 27th parachute troops occupied the town and isthmus of Corinth. The pictures show: above, boatloads of Nazis being hauled from the Greek mainland to occupy Euboea; below, left, German motorcyclists passing through Corinth and, right, Nazi paratroops in action.

German victory parade in the shadow of the Acropolis

NAZIS IN GREEK CAPITAL. Though Athens itself was not the victim of air attack by the Germans, possibly in view of the R.A.F.'s warning that such an exploit would be followed by the bombing of Rome, its suburbs were a target for the Luftwaffe on April 22 and 25. The occupation of the capital on April 27 was celebrated by a great parade of German and Italian troops. Left, German (above) and Italian (below) motorized detachments saluting General List. Right, German infantry marching, with the Acropolis in the background.

HEROES OF THE GREEK WITHDRAWAL BACK IN AFRICA. The British troops operating in Greece were nearly all seasoned veterans of the campaign in Africa. They had been mainly drawn from the Army of the Nile, and on their evacuation returned to Egypt. The picture above shows a transport-load of Anzac and

British Tommies who have just landed at an Egyptian port after their heroic rearguard fight and hazardous crossing of the Mediterranean. They are resting on the docks and appear to be little affected by the grueling experiences they have just undergone.

AIR FORCE HELP IN GREEK WITHDRAWAL. Magnificent work was done during the Greek evacuation by the R.A.F.'s flying boats, which picked up heavy loads of airmen and others from outlying stations from which they could not have reached the embarkation points. One boat took off a load of seventy-two men, fighting off an enemy attack during its journey. Above: R.A.F. personnel being rowed out to a Sunderland flying boat; below: R.A.F. ground staff assembling in trucks to be taken to a port for embarkation.

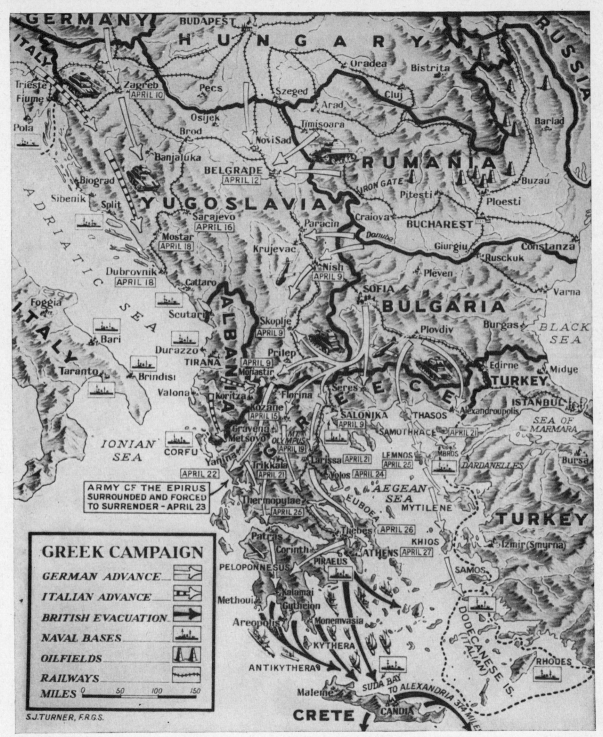

THE TIME TABLE FOR GREECE. Germany's occupation of Rumania and Bulgaria, and Yugoslavia's refusal to join the Axis, hastened the attack upon Greece. The Germans advanced across the Vardar to Monastir and to Salonika. Yugoslavia was isolated and the Greeks in Albania were threatened. British help could not prevent the Nazis reaching Yanina and forcing the surrender of the Greek Army of the Epirus. The allies were pushed back to the Thermopylae line. The loss of air bases in Larissa forced evacuation.

British block Nazi attempt to gain control of Iraq

ANTI-BRITISH MOVEMENT CRUSHED. On May 2 a clash occurred between British forces and Iraq troops concentrated at the R.A.F. station at Habbaniyah, near Baghdad. Under the orders of Raschid Ali, the pro-Nazi premier, who had seized power in Iraq a month previously, troops fired on the airfield, destroying British aircraft. The British bombed the rebel troops and with the assistance of loyal Iraqis expelled them from their positions, at the same time attacking other airfields where trouble had broken out and destroying a great part of the Iraqi air force. Rutbah, an important air station on the oil line and

motor road to Palestine, which had been occupied by the rebels, was retaken by the British on May 10 after an ultimatum had been dropped by the R.A.F. calling for surrender within an hour. The pictures show: below, left, a cavalry squadron of the Transjordan Arab Legion, recruited almost entirely from Bedouin Arabs, moving out of their camp for patrol duties in the desert; this force assisted the British in their action against the Iraqi rebels. Top, left, armored car crew of the Arab Legion's desert patrol. Above, armored car company of the R.A.F. advancing into Iraq after the capture of the fort at Rutbah.

445

German atrocities in occupied Poland

REIGN OF TERROR IN POLAND. Speaking to an American audience on May 9, Lord Halifax, the British Ambassador to Washington, told how the German authorities of the "General Government," the occupied area of Poland, were subjecting the conquered population to a new wave of terror. More than 40,000 Poles, he said, had in all probability been murdered during the few months preceding, and Polish villages were the daily scene of mass floggings and terror reprisals of every kind. These pictures of scenes that were typical of many show: below, left, Polish civilians digging graves for their fellow-countrymen whose bodies lie beside them; right, the hanging bodies of two Poles who have fallen foul of the occupying forces; above, right, Polish prisoners facing a firing squad; left, men on way to execution.

House of Commons and City of London damaged in air raid

LONDON'S SEVEREST AIR RAID. On the full-moon night of May 10, after an almost raid-free three weeks, London endured an intense air attack lasting for several hours, resulting in many casualties and heavy destruction. Vast numbers of incendiaries were dropped, as well as high explosive bombs, and among the killed were the mayors of two London boroughs. The Houses of Parliament were severely damaged, the Commons' debating chamber being wrecked, but the Commons met the following morning in a building

which had been prepared for such an emergency. Westminster Abbey and the British Museum, and many commercial offices and private houses in the City and suburbs, as well as five hospitals, churches, and other public buildings, were hit or burnt out during the raid. Thirty-three enemy planes were brought down—the largest number ever secured in night fighting over England. Left, Mr. Churchill inspects the ruins of Parliament; above, a view from Ludgate Circus, looking towards St. Paul's, the morning after.

449

More historic London buildings battered by the Nazi bombers

MAY RAID DAMAGE IN LONDON. These pictures show some of the results of the great air raid of May 10. Top, left, the famous bells of St. Clement Danes, Strand, celebrated in nursery rhyme, being moved to safety. The church was reduced to a shell in a previous raid. Center, firemen at work in Pilgrim Street, close to St. Paul's on the morning of the raid. Right, Crown Office Row, in the Temple,

where most of the buildings, including the world-famous round Norman Temple Church, suffered severely. Below, left, results of a bomb that fell in the Central Criminal Court, Old Bailey. Center, damaged cloisters at Westminster Abbey; right, the wrecked interior of Westminster Upper School, once the monks' dormitory, where the traditional ceremony of "tossing the pancake" took place.

British night fighters take the measure of the Nazi raiders

BRITAIN'S "SECRET WEAPON" PROVES ITS WORTH. During April night fighters of the R.A.F. began to take serious toll of the German bombers, and by the end of the month they had accounted for fifty out of a record total of eighty-eight destroyed. These figures, however, were soon to be beaten, and on May 4 thirteen of the enemy fell to their guns. Three nights later they destroyed a further twenty-four, but on May 11 they broke all records by shooting down a grand total of thirty-three. The increase in night fighter "kills" was largely due to "Radiolocation," Britain's "secret weapon" which, by the spring of 1941 had reached such a state of perfection that raiding by night became a very risky business for the German bombers. The pictures show: top, left, W.A.A.F. girls in a subterranean operations room plotting the courses of enemy aircraft on a huge map; bottom, left, night fighter pilots walking to their machines before taking off; right, above, a Hurricane night fighter, and, below, a Blenheim night fighter about to set off on patrol.

THE NUMBER THREE NAZI BAILS OUT. The world was astounded to learn on May 12 that Rudolf Hess, Deputy Fuehrer of Germany, had landed near Glasgow by parachute after flying from Germany in a Messerschmitt 110. No official explanation of his desertion was issued, but the general view was that Hess's flight indicated a serious breach of solidarity in the Nazi party, possibly on the question of Russo-German relations. He was treated in Britain as a prisoner of war. Above, Hess, in cockpit, is seen saying good-bye to his wife before taking off on a flight. Below, the wreckage of the plane in which he escaped.

FRANCO-GERMAN AGREEMENT. On May 6 Admiral Darlan and Herr Abetz, German representative in France, signed an agreement providing for certain "concessions" in the occupation terms, and on May 15 it was announced that the French authorities were allowing German planes to use Syrian airfields. The picture above shows the men of Vichy at a ministerial council. Marshal Petain, the Premier, is seen on the left of the picture and seated opposite him is Admiral Darlan, the man who negotiated the agreement with the Nazis. Below, the aged Marshal greeted by the crowd during a memorial service for veterans.

The end of main Italian resistance in Abyssinia

DUKE OF AOSTA SURRENDERS. A culminating point in the East African operations was marked by the surrender on 19 May at Amba Alagi of an Italian army 18,000-19,000 strong. The Duke of Aosta, Viceroy of Abyssinia and Commander-in-Chief of the Italian forces in East Africa, with five generals and a number of his staff officers, was the last to surrender. He is seen in the upper photograph, accompanied by British officers, walking down from the cave which he had used for some time as his headquarters. Below, his

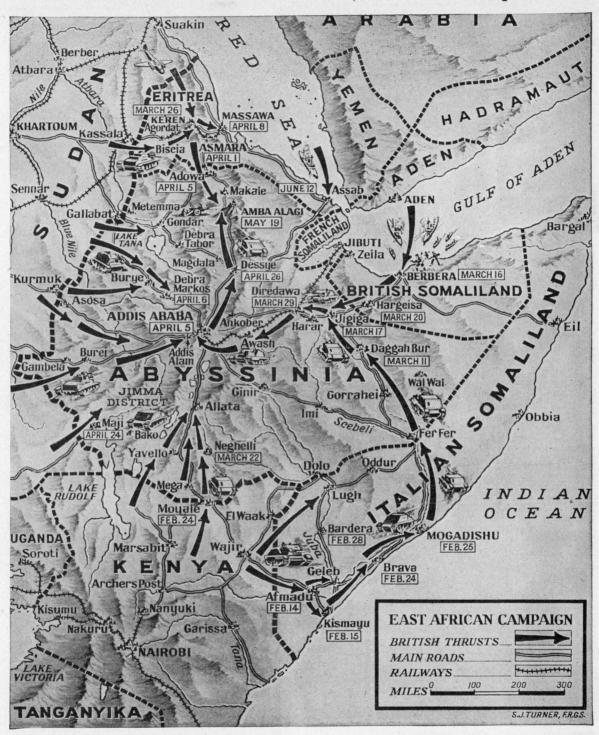

defeated forces are accorded the honors of war by the Transvaal Scottish Regiment. The course of the operations in Abyssinia is indicated on the map on the right. In spite of the difficult country it took the British forces only ninety-four days to cover the 1,500 miles to Amba Alaqi. British, Indian and South African troops shared in the operations which were crowned by the Duke's surrender and thus Mussolini's dream of empire for the Italians was shattered. Italian troops had entered Ethiopia in 1934.

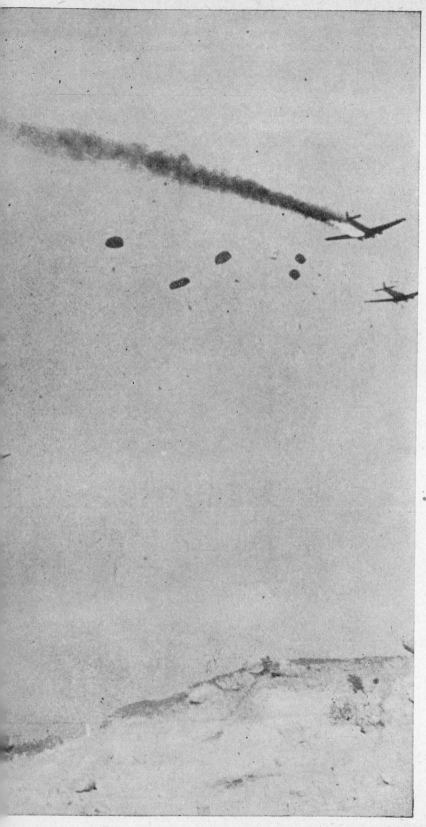

GERMAN AIRBORNE ATTACK ON CRETE

MAY 20, 1941

Having taken possession of the whole of the Greek mainland, the Germans, on May 20, launched a strong air-borne attack on Crete, the Greek island lying across the mouth of the Aegean Sea. This island was of considerable strategic importance to the enemy who wished to establish air bases there for attacks on British shipping in the Mediterranean and also for possible attempts to establish advance bases in Syria and Iraq. The assault on Crete, launched early in the morning, began with violent bombing attacks, followed by mass troop landings by parachute in the neighborhood of Maleme and Heraklion airfields. Later, gliders towed in "trains" behind bombers, and troop-carrying planes and seaplanes landed thousands of troops. The British and Greek forces on the island accounted for a high proportion of the invaders, but the enemy threw in their men regardless of cost and gained a firm foothold at Maleme, to the west of the island. The picture shows parachute troops and equipment descending in the neighborhood of Heraklion airfield; one of the enemy planes is on fire after having been hit by the defending ground forces.

Destruction of troop-carriers and gliders at Maleme

COST OF MALEME CAPTURE. In view of the great disadvantage under which R.A.F. fighters were operating when the attack on Crete was launched, it was decided to withdraw them and leave the defense of the island to land-troops. Unhindered by fighter opposition the enemy were able to land troops in large numbers, and at one period troop-carrying planes at Maleme alone were arriving at the rate of one a minute. Nevertheless enemy casualties were heavy, hundreds of their planes being shot down by the British Fleet lying off the island and by the ground defenses. In addition British bombers, escorted by long-range fighters, raided the occupied airfields and damaged many enemy planes on the ground. The pictures above, taken by British planes, show the airfield at Maleme strewn with damaged planes. Many of these were wrecked by crash-landings; others damaged by British bombs. Below, a destroyed glider is shown.

The Hood goes down in an engagement with the German fleet

BRITAIN'S LARGEST BATTLE CRUISER LOST. On May 22 reconnaissance craft of the British Coastal Command reported that a German battleship and cruiser previously located in Bergen had sailed, and naval forces were at once ordered to intercept them. On the evening of May 23 the enemy were sighted and throughout the night were shadowed by H.M.S. Norfolk and Suffolk. Early the following morning the battleship Prince of Wales and the Battle Cruiser Hood engaged the enemy and during the action that followed the latter received a hit in the magazine and sank, taking with her all but three of her crew.

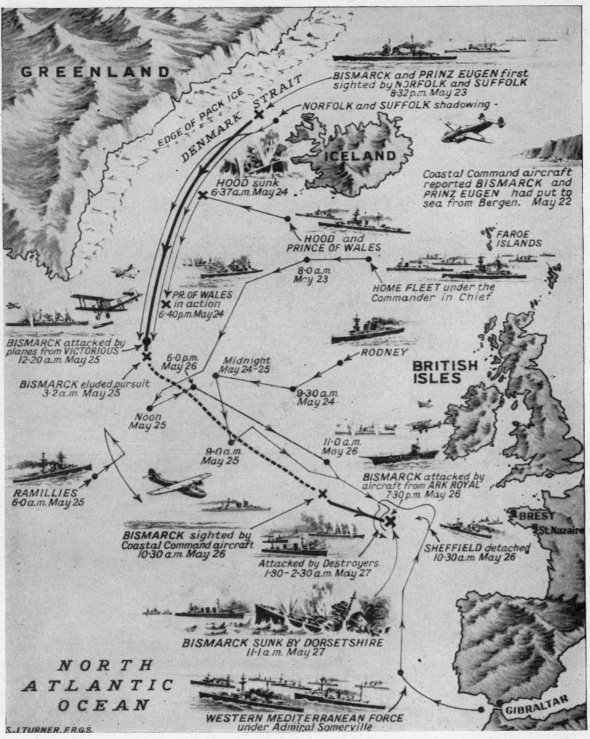

GREENLAND

ICELAND

BRITISH
ISLES

BISMARCK and *PRINZ EUGEN* first
sighted by *NORFOLK* and *SUFFOLK*
8.32 p.m. May 23

NORFOLK and *SUFFOLK* shadowing -

*Coastal Command aircraft
reported BISMARCK and
PRINZ EUGEN had put to
sea from Bergen. May 22*

HOOD sunk
6.37 a.m. May 24

HOOD and
PRINCE OF WALES

8·0 a.m.
May 23

*FAROE
ISLANDS*

HOME FLEET *under the
Commander in Chief*

PR. OF WALES
in action
6.40p.m.May 24

*BISMARCK attacked by
planes from VICTORIOUS
12·20 a.m. May 25*

6·0 p.m.
May 26

Midnight
May 24-25

RODNEY

*BISMARCK eluded pursuit
3·2 a.m. May 25*

8·30 a.m.
May 24

Noon
May 25

9·0 a.m.
May 25

11·0 a.m.
May 26

*BISMARCK attacked by
aircraft from ARK ROYAL
7.30 p.m. May 26*

RAMILLIES
6·0 a.m. May 25

BREST
St. Nazaire

*BISMARCK sighted by
Coastal Command aircraft
10·30 a.m. May 26*

*SHEFFIELD detached
10·30 a.m. May 26*

Attacked by Destroyers
1·30 - 2·30 a.m. May 27

*NORTH
ATLANTIC
OCEAN*

*BISMARCK SUNK BY DORSETSHIRE
11·1 a.m. May 27*

GIBRALTAR

WESTERN MEDITERRANEAN FORCE
under Admiral Somerville

S.J.TURNER. F.R.G.S.

The enemy ships turned out to be the Bismarck, Germany's newest battleship, and the heavy cruiser,
Prinz Eugen, both of which became the subject of an epic chase for revenge. The picture on left, taken
from the deck of H.M.S. Prince of Wales, was the last ever to be taken of H.M.S. Hood. The map on the
right shows pictorially the stages of the thrilling seventeen-hundred-mile chase which resulted, as told
on Pages 464, 465, in the destruction of the Bismarck.

Germany's newest battleship sunk by the British navy

THE HOOD REVENGED. After the sinking of the Hood, British cruisers maintained contact with the Bismarck, whose speed seemed somewhat reduced. On the night of May 24 she was attacked by planes from the aircraft carrier Victorious, which scored a hit, but early the next morning touch was lost. Other units joined in the chase, assisted by R.A.F. planes, and she was again located 550 miles west of Land's End on May 26. Planes from the Ark Royal attacked her twice in the afternoon, scored hits and reduced her

speed. On the morning of the 27th, after a 1,750-mile chase, she was engaged by battleships and sunk by a torpedo from H.M.S. Dorsetshire, the original intention to sink her by gunfire having to be abandoned owing to poor visibility. The pictures show: left, Bismarck seen from a British battleship immediately before the fatal torpedo was launched; above, members of the crew of the German ship struggling in the water; below, the Bismarck just after being hit by the first of the Dorsetshire's torpedoes.

Germans strengthen their foothold on the island of Crete

BITTER FIGHTING IN CRETE. On the night of May 21 the Germans endeavored to reinforce their air-borne troops in Crete by a landing from the sea. This was intercepted by the navy which sank an Italian destroyer, two transports and a number of Greek caiques. In the picture, left, survivors of the convoy are seen being rescued by a British destroyer. In spite of this success, the Germans continued to reinforce their troops by air; by May 26 the enemy had become so strong that the British and Greek troops were compelled to retire from the Canea area, and on May 28 to the east of Suda Bay. Meanwhile Italian air-borne landings were made on the east of the island. Bitter hand-to-hand combats on land were fought by the opposing forces under continuous German dive bombing attacks from the air. The German photograph reproduced above shows Nazi troops in Crete unloading motor cycles and sidecars from a Junkers Ju 52 transport plane.

End of the campaign in Crete—Allied troops evacuated

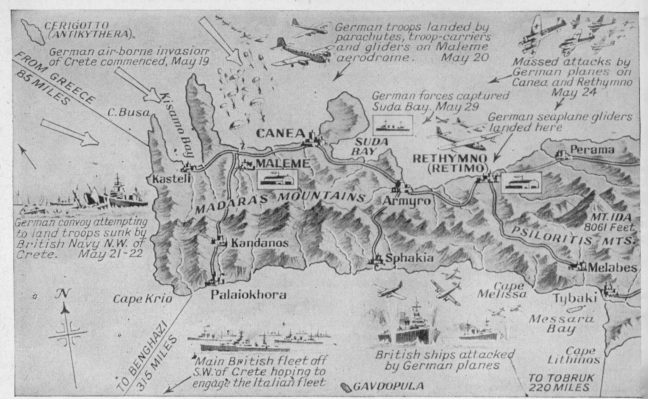

ALLIED TROOPS LEAVE CRETE. By May 31 the Germans in Crete had been so strongly reinforced from the air that further resistance by the Allies became impossible and it was decided to withdraw the troops from the island. Air power had again tipped the balance in the enemy's favor for without adequate air support the Allied troops were subject to constant bombing and were unable to obtain enough rest to keep

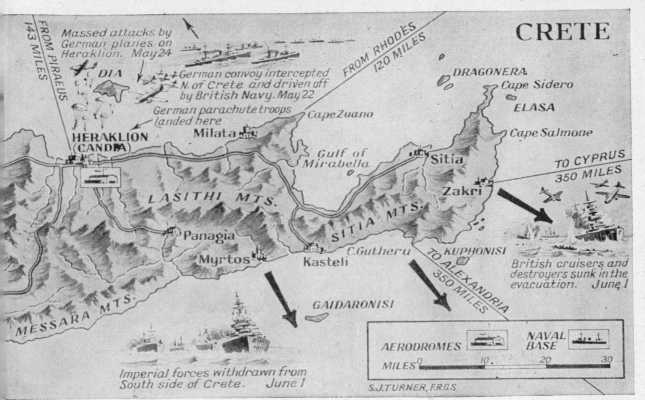

CRETE

Massed attacks by German planes on Heraklion. May 24

German convoy intercepted N. of Crete and driven off by British Navy. May 22

German parachute troops landed here

FROM PIRAEUS 143 MILES

FROM RHODES 120 MILES

DIA

HERAKLION (CANDIA)

Milata

Cape Zuano

Gulf of Mirabella

LASITHI MTS.

SITIA MTS.

Panagia

Myrtos

Kasteli

C. Gutheru

MESSARA MTS.

GAIDARONISI

KUPHONISI

DRAGONERA

Cape Sidero

ELASA

Cape Salmone

Sitia

Zakri

TO CYPRUS 350 MILES

British cruisers and destroyers sunk in the evacuation. June 1

TO ALEXANDRIA 350 MILES

Imperial forces withdrawn from South side of Crete. June 1

AERODROMES   NAVAL BASE

MILES 0   10   20   30

S.J.TURNER, F.R.G.S.

them in good fighting condition. Evacuation began on June 1 and, in spite of violent air attacks, the Navy took off more than 17,000 men for the loss of four cruisers and six destroyers. The course of the campaign is depicted pictorially in the map. The pictures show: left, an enemy dive bombing attack on shipping in Suda Bay; right, smoke rising from allied munition dumps destroyed before the evacuation.

7 JUNE, 1941. LOW-LEVEL ATTACK ON ENEMY CONVOY. In the early summer of 1941 the R.A.F. began to take the offensive, and sweeps by fighters and bombers were made almost daily over occupied France and the North Sea. In the picture above Blenheims of the Bomber Command are launching a mast-high attack on an enemy convoy off the Dutch coast. A bomb can be seen bursting close to the stern of the nearest vessel.

British and Free French forces enter Syria

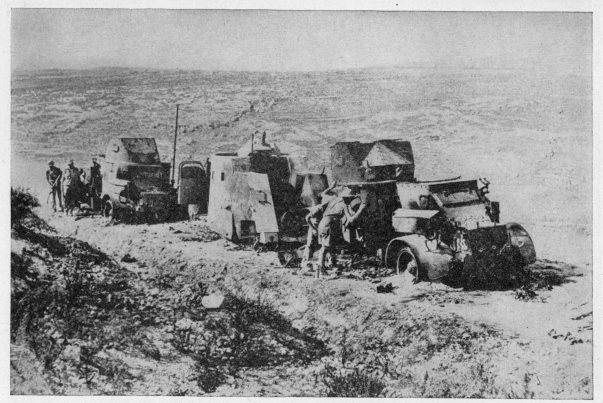

ALLIES CROSS SYRIAN BORDER. On June 8, British and Imperial forces under Sir Henry Maitland Wilson, co-operating with Free French troops under General Catroux, crossed from Palestine and Transjordan into Syria to prevent the Germans, with the connivance of Vichy, securing a hold on that French-mandated territory. Little resistance was encountered at the beginning of the march, which was supported

by leaflet-dropping aircraft. The British commander, anxious to inflict as few casualties as possible upon Britain's former allies, ordered his troops to use force only where absolutely necessary. The pictures show: left, above, Australian infantry marching across typical Syrian country; below, shelled and burnt-out Vichy armored vehicles; right, Australian troops moving cautiously up a hillside during the advance.

THE MARCH INTO SYRIA. Tyre was occupied on the second day of the march into Syria, and the general reaction of the Arabs to the Allied move was favorable, although considerable resistance was offered in some sections, especially at Merj Ayoun, captured by the Australians on June 12. The outskirts of Sidon were reached on the 14th and the town occupied on the 15th. Above, Australian troops, who distinguished themselves during the advance, are in the old Crusaders' castle which they have just cleared.

INFANTRY AND ARTILLERY IN ACTION IN SYRIA. After the fall of Sidon the advance along the coast continued towards Beirut. Meanwhile, in the central sector, considerable resistance was encountered which slowed down the advance towards Damascus. By June 18, however, the encirclement of the capital was almost complete and on the following day advance forces penetrated the suburbs. The pictures show, above, British artillery in action at night, and, below, infantry taking cover behind anti-tank obstacles.

The Allies enter the world's oldest city

DAMASCUS OCCUPIED. Free French troops approached Damascus on the 17th of June and the next day were within three miles of the city. On the 19th General Wilson called on General Dentz, commander of the garrison, to withdraw his men, but the appeal was rejected and the city attacked by Free French and Indian troops, who occupied it after its evacuation on the 21st. Left, above, natives watch the entry of Free French troops in trucks; below, French shells falling close to the British Brigade headquarters outside the city. Right, Generals Catroux and Legentilhomme (in closed car) drive through the city.

A PACT BECOMES A SCRAP OF PAPER. Suddenly and without warning the military might of Germany was hurled against Russia at dawn on June 22, 1941. By this new act of aggression Hitler reversed the policy he initiated one year and ten months previously when he signed a pact of non-aggression with

the Soviet Union. When the Nazis attacked Russia they embarked upon an adventure the outcome of which no one could foretell. That country, covering an area of more than 8,000,000 square miles had, within a quarter of a century, developed from an almost feudal state into a highly industrialized nation.

Soviet air forces slows up advancing German columns

NAZI HORDES ON THE MARCH. The German attack on Soviet Russia was launched along the whole of the front from the Baltic to the Black Sea, with three main drives directed, in the north through the Baltic States towards Leningrad, in the center of Poland through Brest-Litovsk, which fell on June 23, and in the south from Rumania through Bessarabia towards the Ukraine. On the 26th Nazi tanks made a successful

break through in the Minsk sector, but the Russians, ably supported by the Red Air Force, contested every foot of ground and inflicted enormous losses on the enemy. The picture shows a Nazi column advancing into Russia, thrown into confusion by air attack by Russian planes. Some of the trucks have dispersed across fields to get clear of the road. A bomb is seen bursting among Nazi vehicles farther along the road.

The capital of White Russia falls to the Germans

MINSK FALLS TO THE ADVANCING NAZIS. The most successful of the German thrusts into Russia was that in the central sector which was directed against Moscow. Here was fought one of the greatest tank battles of the war in which more than 4,000 tanks took part. On June 26 the enemy succeeded in breaking through the Russian defenses and four days later announced the capture of Minsk. The Russian plan of campaign was to allow the enemy mechanized spearheads to penetrate their lines without offering

resistance and then to close the gap, thereby isolating the fighting vehicles from their supporting infantry. By this means the Russians, during the first week of the war, claimed to have destroyed 2,500 tanks and to have taken more than 30,000 prisoners. The pictures show: above, left, tanks entering Minsk along a street of burnt and blown-up buildings; below, tanks in the center of the town; right, a Russian father, fugitive from the Germans, waits with his child in his arms as his wife lies exhausted on the pavement.

PALMYRA IS OCCUPIED. British and Free French troops began to close in on the ruined desert city of Palmyra on the 26th of June. The city, important because of its position on the oil pipe-line to Tripoli, was stubbornly defended by Vichy troops and hired Arab snipers who, however, were forced to retire and on July 3 the allied troops marched in. Above, a Bren gun carrier is seen among the ruins of the old Roman Colonnade. The crew is hastily alighting to deal with any pockets of resistance that remain.

RUSSIA, TOO, HAS ITS PANZER DIVISIONS. The U.S.S.R., which had for years been mechanizing its army with an eye on a possible German attack, met the onslaught of the Panzer divisions with an armored force in no way inferior to that of the attacker. The pictures show: above, Red Army tanks moving up to the front through heavily-wooded country; they are camouflaged with branches of trees to safeguard them against observation or bombing attack; below, Russian officers of a tank column conferring at the front.

Germans advance in White Russia—the Beresina is crossed

THE SHOCK TROOPS PUSH ON. The Nazi drive in the Minsk sector reached the Beresina River at several points on July 3, but it was not until several days later that the enemy effected a crossing. The picture shows German advance units preparing to force a crossing of the river by means of rafts. The blazing

buildings on the far bank have been set on fire by the retreating Russians who destroyed everything that could be of any possible use to the enemy before falling back to defense lines that had been prepared in advance. This policy prevented the enemy from living on the land and taxed their lines to the utmost.

Syria comes under control of the Allied armies

CEASE FIRING SOUNDED. Hostilities in Syria ended at midnight on July 12-13, after a five weeks' campaign, the course of which is shown on the map. On that day General Dentz's plenipotentiaries signed at Acre the armistice terms offered them by the Free French and British commanders. These terms had been transmitted to Vichy via Washington on the 11th, but had been rejected on the grounds that it was impossible for the French Government to negotiate with the followers of General de Gaulle. General

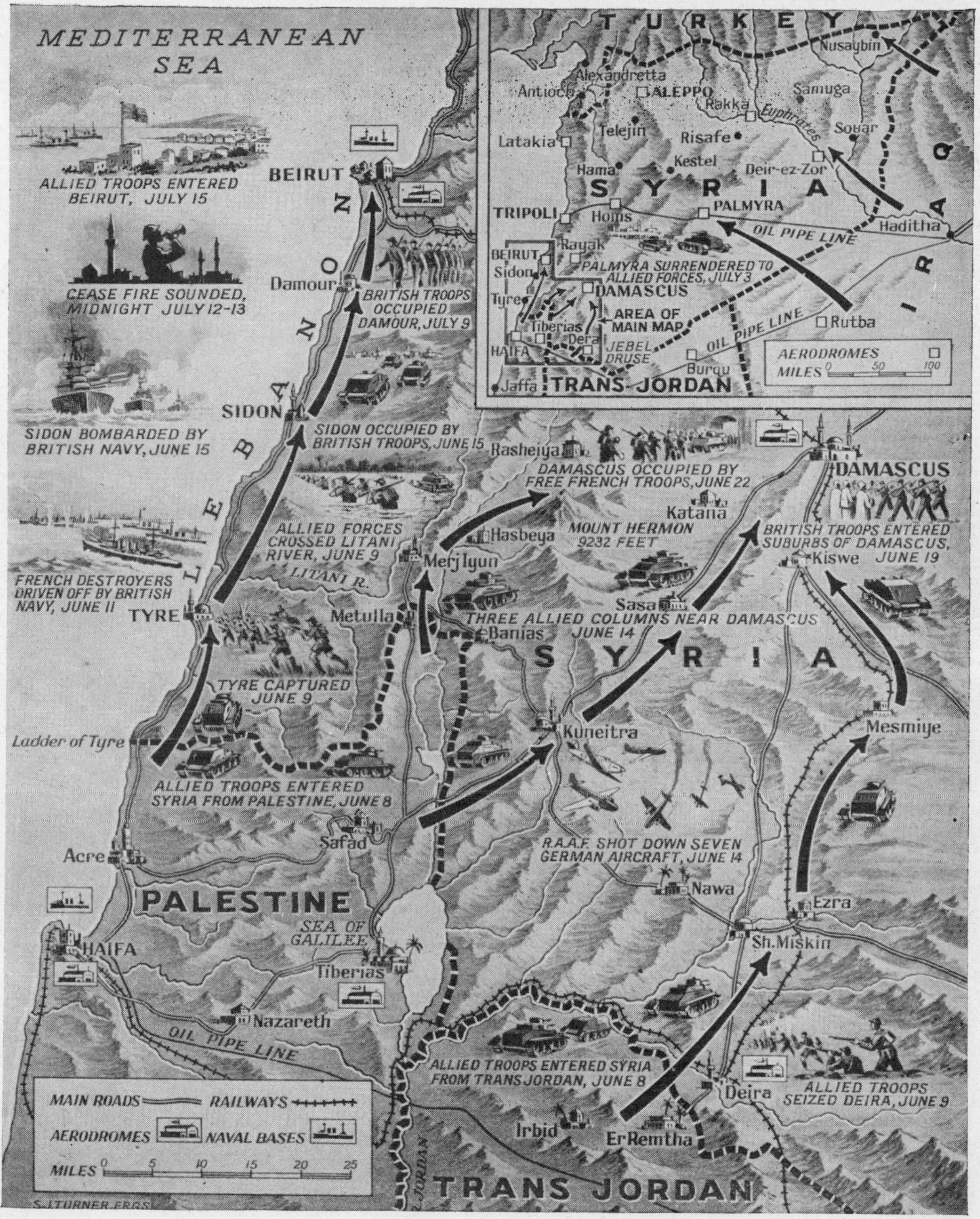

MEDITERRANEAN SEA
ALLIED TROOPS ENTERED BEIRUT, JULY 15
CEASE FIRE SOUNDED, MIDNIGHT JULY 12-13
SIDON BOMBARDED BY BRITISH NAVY, JUNE 15
FRENCH DESTROYERS DRIVEN OFF BY BRITISH NAVY, JUNE 11
BEIRUT
Damour
BRITISH TROOPS OCCUPIED DAMOUR, JULY 9
SIDON
SIDON OCCUPIED BY BRITISH TROOPS, JUNE 15
LEBANON
ALLIED FORCES CROSSED LITANI RIVER, JUNE 9
LITANI R.
TYRE
TYRE CAPTURED JUNE 9
Ladder of Tyre
ALLIED TROOPS ENTERED SYRIA FROM PALESTINE, JUNE 8
Metulla
Merj Iyun
Hasbeya
Banias
Rasheiya
DAMASCUS OCCUPIED BY FREE FRENCH TROOPS, JUNE 22
MOUNT HERMON 9232 FEET
Katana
DAMASCUS
BRITISH TROOPS ENTERED SUBURBS OF DAMASCUS, JUNE 19
Kiswe
Sasa
THREE ALLIED COLUMNS NEAR DAMASCUS JUNE 14
SYRIA
Kuneitra
Mesmiye
R.A.A.F. SHOT DOWN SEVEN GERMAN AIRCRAFT, JUNE 14
Safad
Acre
PALESTINE
SEA OF GALILEE
HAIFA
Tiberias
Nazareth
OIL PIPE LINE
Nawa
Ezra
Sh. Miskin
ALLIED TROOPS ENTERED SYRIA FROM TRANS JORDAN, JUNE 8
Deira
ALLIED TROOPS SEIZED DEIRA, JUNE 9
Irbid
Er Remtha
JORDAN
TRANS JORDAN
MAIN ROADS
RAILWAYS
AERODROMES
NAVAL BASES
MILES 0 5 10 15 20 25
S. J. TURNER F.R.G.S.
TURKEY
Nusaybin
Alexandretta
Antioch
ALEPPO
Samuga
Rakka
Euphrates
Latakia
Telejin
Risafe
Souar
Hama
Kestel
Deir-ez-Zor
SYRIA
IRAQ
TRIPOLI
Homs
PALMYRA
Haditha
OIL PIPE LINE
Rayak
BEIRUT
Sidon
PALMYRA SURRENDERED TO ALLIED FORCES, JULY 3
Tyre
DAMASCUS
AREA OF MAIN MAP
Tiberias
Dera
Rutba
HAIFA
JEBEL DRUSE
Burqu
Jaffa
TRANS-JORDAN
AERODROMES
MILES 0 50 100

Dentz, however, as commander on the spot, was given a free hand to decide whether or not to continue hostilities. In the lower picture the Vichy envoy is seen leaving British forward divisional headquarters after having discussed armistice terms with the British commander. Above, General Sir Henry Maitland Wilson, with the Free French General Catroux on his right, is seen signing the treaty on behalf of Great Britain. More than 1,000 British troops were either killed or wounded in the campaign.

A NEW TREATY IS SIGNED. On July 9, a Russian mission arrived in London to discuss common action to be taken against Germany by the two countries. Above, M. Maisky, Soviet Ambassador to the Court of St. James's, is seen with General Golikov (light tunic), Rear Admiral Kharlamov (behind him) and other members of the mission on their arrival. Four days later in Moscow, Sir Stafford Cripps, British Ambassador to the U.S.S.R. (below), signed, on behalf of Britain, a pact of mutual assistance.

RESULTS OF A DAYLIGHT ATTACK. Representative of the continual attacks by the R.A.F. on northern France and other enemy-occupied countries was an attack in early July on Comines in daylight. Its results are visible above. The principal objective was the electric power station and direct hits were scored on the boiler house, pump house and circulating water-pipe system, while several near misses caused additional damage. Direct hits were also scored on the buildings in the area marked by a dotted line.

Blenheim aircraft bomb Rotterdam in a daylight raid

HOLLAND WELCOMES BRITISH BOMBERS. A highly successful daylight attack on Rotterdam Harbor on July 16 by Blenheim aircraft resulted in the putting out of action of seventeen enemy ships, totaling nearly 100,000 tons, while five other vessels were severely damaged. The planes, operating at mast-high level amid the cheers of the Dutch onlookers, also fired two large warehouses and a factory. Left, above, bursting bombs along the dockside as observed from one of the attacking planes, whose tail is seen in the left foreground; right, Dutch passers-by wave greetings to the Blenheims from a Rotterdam suburb, a striking tribute to the bomb-aiming ability of the British airmen. Below, three of the Blenheims are seen flying low over the roof-tops as they "hedge-hop" their way home after the attack.

SYRIAN SEAPORT OCCUPIED BY ALLIES. The formal entry of the Allied troops, Australian, Indian, British and Free French, into Beirut, as provided for by the Syrian Armistice, took place on July 15. The democratic forces received a hearty welcome from the dense crowds of inhabitants who lined the streets to cheer them (above) as their transport and guns entered the lovely city. Below are seen Australian infantry, first of the Allied forces to enter the liberated city, marching to the Place de Martyrs.

EMPIRE READY IN FAR EAST. The thickening of the storm-clouds in the Far East, following on the fear of Japanese action against Indo-China and Thailand, led in July to the tightening-up of Imperial defenses in Malaya, where large reinforcements of British and Indian troops and R.A.F. personnel arrived to reinforce the garrison. Above, Australian transport and Bren gun carriers crossing a Malayan bridge on maneuvres; below, men of a famous regiment on the march through tropical country in the peninsula.

America comes a step closer to the Second World War

AMERICANS ARRIVE IN ICELAND. Members of the United States Infantry going ashore in tenders from their transports upon their arrival in Iceland to garrison the island with British troops.

WELCOME FROM TOMMY ATKINS. An American doughboy (left) being greeted by a British soldier as the American forces arrived in Iceland. Later the British were evacuated.

NEWS FROM THE STATES. American troops in Iceland reading the first issue of the newspaper produced for the troops garrisoned in the Atlantic outpost to keep open the Lend-lease supply line.

A PLACE TO KEEP WARM. American and British soldiers working shoulder to shoulder building huts for the American contingent on the island notorious for its bad weather.

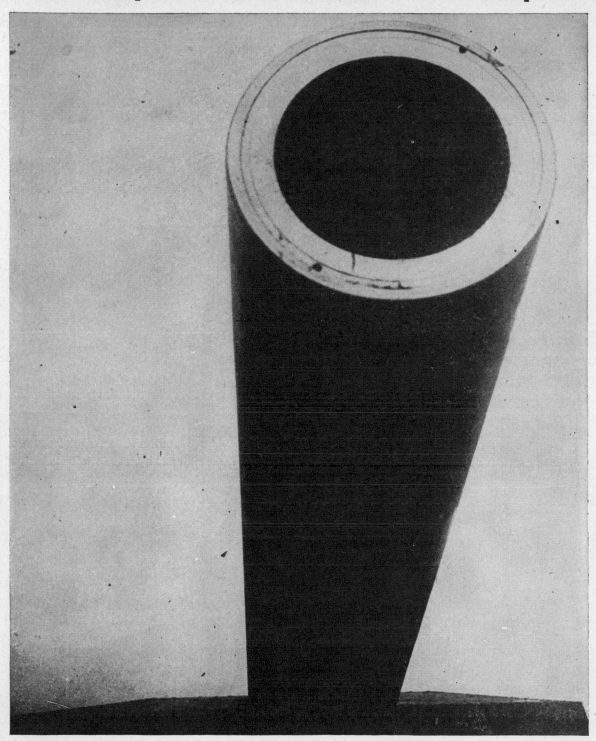

BIRD'S-EYE VIEW. Looking down the long barrel of one of the long-range siege guns on the French Coast with which the Nazis hammered at the English Coast and at shipping in the Channel. These guns were installed after the fall of France and were used intermittently during the German occupation. They caused considerable damage to property in Dover and other English coastal towns.

THREAT TO MOSCOW EASED. After crossing the Beresina, the Nazis pushed on towards Smolensk, a vital junction on the railway to Moscow. Here, Russian counter-attacks brought the offensive to a standstill and inflicted huge losses on the invaders. In these operations the Luftwaffe found its match in the Red Air Force and ground defenses, which together accounted for hundreds of German bombers. Above, Soviet A.A. guns in action; the smoke shows that one bomber, at least, will trouble them no more.

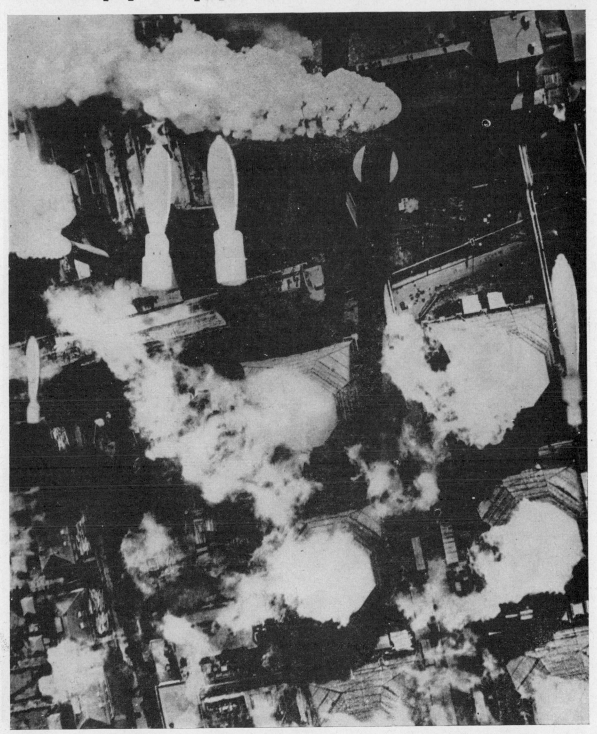

ATTACK ON THE RHINELAND. One of the most daring attacks of the war was made by Blenheim bombers of the R.A.F., when they attacked power stations at Cologne, almost at ground level, on August 12. Many direct hits were scored in the face of heavy fire from the ground defenses and huge fires were left burning in the target area. Twelve bombers and eight fighter planes were lost in these operations. Above, a salvo of bombs falling on the Knapsack Power Station, the largest steam power plant in Europe.

Germans break through in the Ukraine as Russians retreat

RUSSIANS RETREAT TOWARDS THE DNIEPER. With their advance in the Central Sector held up, the Germans redoubled their attacks in the Ukraine. They hoped to encircle Marshal Budenny's southern army, but the Russians withdrew in good order. On the 14th they were forced to abandon Permovaisk, and two days later, after destroying the dock installations, they evacuated Nikolayev. Odessa, though encircled, still held out as the Russian armies fell back towards the Dnieper. The pictures show: top, left, motor cyclists advancing along a Ukrainian road, and, right, crossing a bridge. Below, left, horse supply wagons, and, right, tanks advancing.

CHURCHILL AND ROOSEVELT MEET

On August 14 it was announced that President Roosevelt and Prime Minister Churchill had met at sea on board H.M.S. Prince of Wales and the U. S. cruiser Augusta. At these meetings they discussed matters of vital importance to the two countries and issued the Atlantic Charter, the eight points are printed below. The pictures show, above and right, the two leaders at a Sunday morning service aboard the Prince of Wales surrounded by the members of their staffs who accompanied them; below, left, Mr. Churchill hands Mr. Roosevelt (on the arm of his son Elliot), a personal letter from King George.

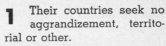

EIGHT POINTS OF

1 Their countries seek no aggrandizement, territorial or other.

2 They desire to see no territorial changes that do not accord with the freely expressed wishes of the peoples concerned.

3 They respect right of all peoples to choose the form of government under which they will live. . . .

4 They will endeavor, with due respect for their existing obligations, to further enjoyment by all States, great or small, victor or vanquished, of access, on equal terms, to the trade and to the raw materials of the world which are needed for their economic prosperity.

5 They desire to bring about fullest collaboration between all nations in economic field. . . .

6 After final destruction of Nazi tyranny, they hope to see established a peace

THE ATLANTIC CHARTER

which will afford to all nations the means of dwelling in safety within their own boundaries. . . .

7 Such a peace should enable all men to traverse the high seas and oceans without hindrance.

8 They believe all of the nations of the world, for realistic as well as spiritual reasons, must come to the abandonment of the use of force.

Since no future peace can be maintained if land, sea or air armaments continue to be employed by nations which threaten, or may threaten, aggression outside of their frontiers, they believe . . . disarmament of such nations is essential.

They will likewise aid and encourage all other practicable measures which will lighten . . . the crushing burden of armament.

GERMAN ADVANCE IN THE EAST. After eight weeks of bitter fighting the main German objectives of Moscow, Leningrad and Kiev were still in Russian hands. During the seventh and eighth weeks, however, the enemy drive in the north threatened to encircle Leningrad, whilst in the central sector, the fall of Smolensk on August 13, brought the enemy nearer to Moscow. In the Ukraine the Russians were forced towards the Dnieper, leaving Kiev at the apex of a dangerous salient. The lines of advance are shown.

GERMAN THREAT TO IRAN REMOVED. After having made several unsuccessful protests to the Iranian Government regarding the presence of an unnecessarily large German colony in that country, Britain and Russia sent troops into Iran on August 25. Their objectives were Teheran, the capital, and the oil wells centered around Abadan (above). Only slight opposition was encountered, and on the 28th, after the fall of the pro-Nazi Government, the Shah ordered troops to cease resisting. On August 31, British and Russian forces met near Kazvin to the north-west of the capital, where courtesies were exchanged between the British and Russian commanders. Map shows lines of the advances.

507

The Germans advance across the wheat fields of the Ukraine

NAZI PUSH IN THE UKRAINE. After the fall of Nikolayev Marshal Budenny's armies fell back in good order towards the broad River Dnieper. On August 17, however, with the object of crossing the river higher up, and outflanking the Russians, the Nazis made a determined thrust at Gomel, half-way between Smolensk and Kiev, but determined counter-attacks by "suicide divisions" held the attackers whilst the retreat farther

south continued. On August 28 the Russians announced the fall of Dnepropetrovsk, the great Ukraine steel city on the west bank of the Dnieper and the blowing up of the remaining bridges. Meanwhile the counter-attack in the Gomel area was gaining ground in spite of heavy reinforcements which the Nazis were throwing in. The picture shows German tanks in the Ukraine crossing wheat fields that have been fired by the Russians.

509

Moscow and Leningrad prepare to resist the enemy

GERMAN ADVANCE THREATENS TWO KEY CITIES. While the battle at Gomel was raging two Nazi thrusts farther north threatened Moscow and Leningrad. The former, a continuation of the Smolensk attack, gained little ground against the stubborn Russian resistance, but the latter made more headway and on August 25 the Russians announced the evacuation of Novgorod, one hundred miles south of Leningrad. On August 27 the enemy claimed that they had cut the Moscow-Leningrad railway, and on September 2 the

Russians announced the fall of Tallinn, in Estonia. While these battles were raging, the people of the two chief cities were preparing to defend their homes to the end. Women in Moscow, like those seen digging anti-tank ditches (left), worked with their menfolk to strengthen the city's defenses in answer to Stalin's appeal to keep the enemy at bay at all costs. The picture above shows the German shock troops advancing amid the flames and smoke of burning buildings in an attempt to penetrate the flexible Russian lines.

MEDITERRANEAN SEA BATTLE. Units of the Italian fleet engaged by British convoy escort on the way from Alexandria to Malta. A cruiser is smoke-screening the convoy while the forward guns of another roar.

OXFORD HONORS A QUEEN IN EXILE. Queen Wilhelmina of the Netherlands inspects a Dutch guard of honor in the quadrangle of Oxford after ceremonies in which she received an honorary degree.